GAUDÍ

Gaudí, with the white beard, and Cardinal Ragonesi on a visit to the Sagrada Familia

GAUDÍ

David Mower

ORESKO BOOKS LTD·LONDON

ACKNOWLEDGEMENTS

The format of this book has necessitated omissions, the most important of which are Gaudí's early religious projects and his restorations of Mallorca Cathedral, 1904–14. I have been unable to visit either Astorga or León and have therefore limited to a minimum discussion of Gaudí's buildings in these places. In the interests of clarity, I have taken the liberty of discussing the Sagrada Familia as a separate issue outside the general chronological development.

I should like to thank Prof. Brian Tate of the Spanish Department, Nottingham University, for re-awakening an interest in Gaudí and David Mackay of the architectural practice Martorell Bohigas Mackay for an interesting conversation in Barcelona.

Prof. Juan Bassegoda, holder of the Catedra Gaudí at the School of Architecture within Barcelona University, was exceptionally generous in giving me his time and knowledge and without his assistance this book would have been deficient in many respects.

My gratitude also goes to Wolfgang Pehnt, who made available to me the text by Finsterlin quoted on page 7 and to my friend Roger Morsley Smith for providing its translation.

Archivo Fotográfico Internacional Salmer, Barcelona and Archivo Mas, Barcelona kindly granted permission for including photographs from their collections, and the Colegio Oficial de Arquitectos de Cataluña y Baleares generously agreed to the reproduction of the plans for which it holds the copyright. Rita Blume of Editorial Blume has also been most helpful.

Finally I thank Mrs. Dorothy Birkett for so patiently and efficiently dealing with my inter-library loan requests and my publisher, Robert Oresko, for commissioning this work.

For my Parents.

First published in Great Britain by
Oresko Books Ltd., 30 Notting Hill Gate, London W.11

ISBN 0 905368 08 8 (cloth)
ISBN 0 905368 09 6 (paper)
Copyright © Oresko Books Ltd. and David Mower 1977

Printed in Great Britain by
Burgess and Son (Abingdon) Ltd., Abingdon, Oxfordshire

Contents

Opinions of Gaudí

'But anyhow Barcelona is American, Neapolitan, Marseillais, and above all art-nouveau—for in no city did that horrible epidemic rage more fiercely than there. There it left its great monument, the still unfinished, and I trust never to be finished, cathedral (sic). I saw it long ago in the hey-day of its creation with one transept accomplished and the choir sketched in, and already it was a show place, with a railing round and a peseta for admittance—already it had all the desolating air of a ruin. On that occasion I was shown the snails cast from life and then enlarged mechanically to 10 feet diameter so as to creep decoratively round the moulding of an arch 50 feet up; I was shown how the Virgin and Child on a donkey had also been cast from life and magnified and deposited in the great rockery up there. This time I only saw its megatherian skeleton from the train, looking by now rather dirty and disconsolate, rather more of a ruin, and rather less of a building, than before.'

Roger Fry, *A Sampler of Castile*
(London, 1923)

'For the first time since I had been in Barcelona I went to look at the cathedral (sic), a modern cathedral, and one of the most hideous buildings in the world. It has four crenellated spires exactly the shape of hock bottles. Unlike most of the churches in Barcelona it was not damaged during the Revolution—it was spared because of its "Artistic value", people said. I think the anarchists showed bad taste in not blowing it up when they had the chance . . . .'

George Orwell, *Homage to Catalonia* (London, 1938)

'The greatest piece of creative architecture in the last twenty-five years. It is spirit symbolised in stone!'

Louis Sullivan quoted by T. E. Tallmadge in *Western Architect,* vol. XXI (March 1922)

'Gaudí, among those [architects] of the old school, has interested me from the point of view of construction. Some of the Sagrada Familia walls are a marvel of technical perfection.'

Walter Gropius quoted in *El Propagador De La Devocion a San Jose,* vol. LXVI (1 June 1932)

'What I had seen in Barcelona was the work of a man of extraordinary force, faith and technical capacity . . . . Gaudí is "the" constructor of 1900, the professional builder in stone, iron or bricks. His glory is acknowledged today in his own country. Gaudí was a great artist. Only they remain and will endure who touch the sensitive hearts of men . . . .'

Le Corbusier, 1957

'As I was looking at the "Flight into Egypt", carved in stone at the entrance of the big portal, and wondering at the ass, creeping along so wearily under its burden, he [Gaudí] said to me: "You know something about art, and you have a sort of feeling that the ass here is not an invention. Not one of the figures you see here in stone is imaginary; they all stand here just as I have seen them in reality, Joseph, Mary, the infant Jesus, the priests in the Temple: I chose them all from people I met, and have carved them from plaster casts which I took at the time. With the donkey it was a difficult job. When it became known that I was looking out for an ass for the 'Flight into Egypt', they brought me all the finest donkeys in Barcelona. But I could not use them. Mary, with the Child Jesus, was not to be mounted on a fine strong animal, but on one poor, old and weary, and surely one which had something kindly in its face and understood what it was all about. Such was the donkey I was looking for, and I found it at last in the cart of a woman who was selling scouring sand. Its drooping head almost touched the ground. With much trouble I persuaded its owner to bring it to me. And then, as it was copied, bit by bit, in plaster of Paris, she kept crying because she thought it would not escape with its life. That is the ass of the 'Flight into Egypt', and it has made an impression on you because it is not imagined, but is from actual life." '

Albert Schweitzer, *Out of my Life and Thought*, translated by C. T. Campion (London, 1933)

'Gaudí has built one house from the forms of the sea, representing storm-tossed waves. Another house is made from the still water of a lake. This is no question of deceptive metaphors or fairy-stories—these houses actually exist, real buildings, real sculpture showing twilight reflections of clouds in water, by means of a huge crazy pointillistic mosaic, shining with many colours. From it emerge the forms of water, widely spreading water, spilt water, stagnant water, shimmering water and water rippled by the wind, all these aspects of water put together in an asymmetrical sequence; a dynamic instantaneous movement of broken syncopated and entwined reliefs melting into "naturalistic-stylised" water lilies . . . erupting from the incredible facade in goosepimples of fear. . . . Erotic desire is the ruin of intellectual aesthetics. When the Venus of logic is burnt out, the Venus of bad-taste . . . announces herself under the sign of unique beauty, the beauty of real agitation, both vital and materialist.'

Salvador Dali, 'De la beauté terrifiante et comestible de l'architecture modern style', *Minotaure,* no. 3/4 (1933)

The German Expressionist architect, Hermann Finsterlin, was in contact with Gaudí c. 1918–19.

'The only thing I can remember out of the short correspondence with Gaudí, that I wanted to make clear to him, was that today it was not a question of dressing or masking the thousand-year-old polyhedron with Gothic, Baroque, Moorish or Indian details in an "Art Nouveau" manner or of altering vaults or pillars, however originally, but of letting the whole building grow from the inside, like a highly complicated fruit . . . like a tropical orchid, a fruit to which man (or God) must adapt himself like a pollinating insect. Artistically

expressed—an abstract, giant, hollow sculpture with the highest exterior and interior aesthetic experiences, endlessly changing like music. I believe I once wrote to Gaudí suggesting that he should sometime erect his chimneys, alcoves and turrets, all the charming details of his last buildings, as large structures on the ground, the same individual forms but bigger . . . .

'The Sagrada Familia is for me one of the building-wonders of the world . . . . Like the Taj Mahal, the Sagrada Familia was no house of God, but a house of the Goddess, of his Goddess, his heavenly and therefore unhappy love. For such cathedrals are only built by a heart in monstrous despair or one in Dionysian ecstasy, and only a superman is capable of such creative despair.'

Hermann Finsterlin, 'Gaudí und ich', a monologue for the 'Amigos de Gaudí', Barcelona, 1967 [?]

A Directory of Gaudí's Work in Barcelona

1. The Citadel Park (1875–81?), Paseo del Borne

2. Lamp posts (1878), Plaza Real

3. The College of Jesus Maria (1879–81), San Paciano parish, Calle Valles 40

4. The Vicens House (1883–85), Calle Carolinas 24–26 (*Metro Lesseps*)

5. The Güell Pavilions (1884–87), Avenida de la Victoria (*Metro Maria Cristina*)

6. The Bocabella altar piece (1885), Ausias March 31

7. The Güell Palace (1885–90), Calle Conde del Asalto (*Metro Liceo*)

8. The Convent of Santa Teresa (1889–94), Granduxer 41

9. The Calvet House (1898–1904), Calle de Caspe 48

10. The Miralles Gateway (1900), Paseo Manuel Girona 53 (*Metro Maria Cristina*)

11. 'Bellesguard' (1900–02), Calle de Bellesguard 23 (*Bonanova suburb*)

12. The Park Güell (1900–14), Calle Ramiro de Maeztu

13. The Batlló House (1904–06), Paseo de Gracia 43 (*Metro Aragón*)

14. The Milá House (1906–10), Paseo de Gracia 92 (*Metro Diagonal*)

15. The Infant School for the Sagrada Familia (1909), Providenza 450

16. The Sagrada Familia (1883–1926), Providenza 450

Gaudí and his Work

'What is Architecture? Surely the crystallized expression of man's noblest thoughts, of his ardour, his human nature, his faith, his religion.'

Walter Gropius, *Pamphlet for Workers Council for Art* (Berlin, 1919)

'The house shelters daydreaming, the house protects the dreamer . . . . The house is one of the greatest powers of integration for the thoughts, memories and dreams of mankind . . . .
The house acquires the physical and moral energy of a human body . . . . Such a house invites mankind to a heroism of cosmic proportions. It is an instrument with which to confront the cosmos.'

Gaston Bachelard, *Poetics of Space* (Paris, 1958)

LITERATURE ON GAUDÍ has often taken sides in two mistaken debates; firstly, whether he is to be regarded as a serious architect or as some kind of nonconformist oddity, and, secondly, whether structure or decoration is to be given greater importance in his work. There has been too much case-making, too many defensive apologies.

The attitude which caused Orwell in *Homage to Catalonia* (1938) to describe the Sagrada Familia as 'hideous', echoing a similar attack by Roger Fry in 1922, the same attitude which made Evelyn Waugh talk of 'Fairy cabins from the worst kind of Rackhamesque Picture Book' can today be seen as hasty insults which offer no challenge.

If ill-considered attacks are no longer in fashion, approval also brings problems. Gaudí's lively vulgarity is in danger of being swamped by uncritical praise as certain critics seek to cut through his mongrel crust to values which they see as more respectable. Gaudí ought not to be co-opted too firmly into the echelons of good taste.

Too often Gaudí has been taken out of real context. Led by Dali, a fellow Catalan, certain sections of Surrealism have attempted to use Gaudí for their own purposes, while critics and historians in the early 1960s, renovating interest in Art Nouveau, have found Gaudí useful in supporting that style's claims to be more than merely a movement in the decorative arts. More recently, the organic approach to architectural design from Aalto to Utzon, including the shell structures of Torroja, Nervi and Candela, has been provided with a history in which Gaudí earns for himself a place by his use of warped surfaces and hyperbolic constructions. There has never

been any lack of writing about Gaudí. The pace of publication, however, increased after the 1952 centenary of his birth and the establishment in Barcelona of the Amigos de Gaudí. Much of this literature has remained inaccessible to an English-speaking public either for linguistic reasons or physical availability.

An Image of Gaudí

Folklore hero, mystic recluse, near-saint, emotional hedgehog, freak, images of Gaudí have been various. The demands of establishing an architectural practice meant that as a young man he went out into society, mixed in artistic and literary circles, dressed well and dined out. Increasingly, however, in his maturity he adopted a reticence in social relationships, a discretion regarding his private life and a reluctance to commit himself to verbal statements. All these things have compounded our general ignorance of Gaudí the man and have inevitably encouraged myth-making based on rumour and gossip.

So often people of great vision or achievement appear smaller than they ought to be. Gaudí's actual presence would have disappointed. He was frail, rheumatic, with a white beard and shaven head. The only signs of an intense inner life came from his piercing blue eyes and what one contemporary described as 'a luminous half-laugh'.

Viewed from outside, his life remained uneventful, self-contained, ruled by routine. He never married and lived, most of his professional life, with his father and orphaned niece. He went through life with the minimum of baggage and so little concerned himself with the patina of wealth and fame that at the time of his fatal accident in 1926, when he was run over by a trolley bus, he was mistaken for a tramp and taken to a pauper's bed in the hospital of Santa Cruz.

His abstention from luxury, the tameness of his private life, a conversion to vegetarianism and an obsessive religious commitment have all contributed to the 'outsider' view of Gaudí. Certainly his religion was lived more fervently than is normal and has occasioned numerous anecdotes, some of which may well be apocryphal. It was a faith which could cause him so to overdo Lenten fasting that friends feared for his life, which could make him mouth the Angelus in the midst of company and which, in 1924, resulted in brief imprisonment when he protested against the police closure of churches.

The routine of his working day began with a visit to Barcelona Cathedral, where he could be seen as early as 5 a.m., and ended with prayers in the oratory of St. Felipe Neri.

Catalonia

There were three beliefs sustaining Gaudí's life: the belief in architecture, the belief in a Christian god and the belief in Catalonia. Catalonia is the area situated in the northeast corner of Spain, centred on the port of Barcelona. Gaudí's career coincided with a period in Catalonia of considerable fermentation and disruption. It is perhaps dangerous to underestimate the complexities of this political circuitry, but in brief, it can be explained as the growth and mixing of two movements: firstly the revival of Catalan nationalism and secondly the appearance of socialism and trade-unionism attending the region's industrial expansion. It was a period of public passion when it was difficult for the individual not to be aware of civic responsibilities. There were divisions, confrontations, but also enormous public spirit.

Mindful of its heroic medieval past, Catalonia had traditionally asserted its difference from Castilian Spain. It never failed to compare its own prosperity and enterprise with the inefficiencies of Madrid. Separatism had begun in the seventeenth century when in the war between Spain and France, Catalonia placed itself under the protection of the French king. Thereafter such defiance simmered, mitigated by the desire to make money, but preserved by linguistic links with southern France and by the geographical position of the region, effectively insulated by mountain ranges.

In the nineteenth century this national independence began to assert itself once more, spurred to action by threats to the economy. In the 1840s Catalan industrialists grouped together to protect their interests against English and French competition. In the 1820s and 1830s, foreseeing danger, the Madrid government attempted to demoralize Catalonia by depriving it of its own penal laws and commercial coinage and by forbidding the use of the Catalan language in schools. Bad psychology merely embittered the Catalans; insults and humiliations would be answered when the time was right. This proved to be

in the late 1870s, when Castile was in disarray after the second Carlist war.

The Catalans had in general sided with the Carlists, and after the defeat of the Carlist pretender to the Spanish throne they used, with typical commercial opportunism, the Carlist propaganda organizations for their own purposes. This was the time to make their own demands as the larger political unit of Spain was then at its most vulnerable. They began a concerted action for national Catalan unity which, in its beginnings, was affiliated to High Church sections of the community, to the right of the political spectrum.

Nationalism was aided not only negatively by the weakness of the political fabric of Spain, but positively by the strength and moral credit amassed by Catalonia in its remarkable industrial and trade expansion. Within less than fifty years, Catalonia had developed into a major industrial area specializing in transport and textile industries. If this was strength, it also brought problems. Successful capitalism was an open target for the spirit of socialism abroad in Europe.

Along with manifestoes demanding home rule, Barcelona in the 1890s heard the first demands for better conditions and shorter hours for workers. Political extremists were able to exploit and use this industrial unrest, and Catalonia periodically erupted in strikes and anarchist bomb-throwing well into the twentieth century, until the establishment of the military dictatorship in 1923. Genuine demands and ideals were slandered, confused through constant corruption and provocation and, ultimately, repressed, sometimes fiercely, by the central government in Madrid.

The Arts in Catalonia

Intellectuals had been encouraging pride in national achievement since the 1850s. A cultural campaign had begun not unnaturally by reviving the Catalan language and its literature. The Jocs Florals was re-established, promoting a new school of spirited indigenous poetry. Catalan plays were produced, and the first newspapers in Catalan appeared. In 1876, the Centre Excursionista promoted interest in sites and buildings of national importance, and a real attempt was started at restoring the region's architectural heritage. In 1891, Orfeó, a choral organization, was founded to advance national unity through music, and in its concerts Catalan folk music was given great importance.

A major opportunity to show off the fruits of this renaissance and to establish new goals was the International Exhibition held in Ciudadela Park, Barcelona, in 1888. One definite result of this was the support given to developing traditional Catalan crafts, ceramics, terracotta, tiles and iron work.

Architecture is usually born of pride. In Barcelona during the 1880s and 1890s, there was a coincidence of wealthy patrons wishing to express personal and civic prestige by commissioning new buildings and a group of young architects eager to play their part in asserting national consciousness. Gaudí, although slightly older, is to be seen in the context of such a group, which at the very least provided him with moral support; men such as Josep Vilaseca (1848–1910), Lluís Doménech i Montaner (1850–1923), Josep Doménech i Estapà (1858–1917), Francesc Berenguer (1866–1914), Josep Puig i Cadafalch (1867–1956), Jeroni F. Granell (1867–1931), Lluís Moncunill (1868–1931), Juan Rubió (1871–1952) and José M. Jujol (1879–1949).

All of these architects shared an exuberance, a searching for originality, an exploitation of colour and a celebration of brick and ceramic. Most of them, however, never quite assimilated stylistic borrowings as successfully as Gaudí. They lacked his continual inventiveness and range and the bold confidence of his grasp of three-dimensional form. Less arrogant than Gaudí, they probably satisfied their clients more often. Their work provides Gaudí's achievement with a frame of reference and mitigates some of his improbability.

Unlike Puig i Cadafalch and Doménech i Montaner, both of whom assumed important civic and political roles, Gaudí remained aloof from direct involvement in the political arena. He joined the Centre Excursionista and attended the lectures of Fontanals, a major figure in the literary revival, but, once a professional, his most committed act was to treat more than one famous visitor to a stream of fluent Catalan, knowing full well they were unable to understand it.

Local self-satisfaction in general was never a danger. Catalonia's trade success had enabled her to make contact with Europe while the rest of Spain withdrew into insularity. In cultural terms, this explains the great sympathy found in Barcelona at the end of the nineteenth century for European ideals. Wagner, Ibsen, Nietzsche, Pre-Raphaelitism, Impressionism, albeit curious bedfellows, all gained interested appreciation from artistic and literary circles. It is important to realize that the very existence of such strong nationalist feelings kept foreign attractions in perspective; there could be no danger of a wholesale sell-out. The élite of Catalonia listened but then continued to seek its own identity. This combination of tolerant openness to outside influence combined with the celebration of national consciousness was uniquely fortuitous. It allowed for the creation of an art form of deep resonance, which accepted the structure of a particular culture while at the same time avoiding the dangers of a parochial backwater.

Gaudí's Early Life

Gaudí was born on 25 June 1852 near Tarragona. The industrial town of Reus and its neighbour Riudoms have been engaged for some time in a verbal tug of war over the distinction of being Gaudí's birthplace. The problem arises because local records of births were not kept at this time. His baptism is recorded in the Church of San Pedro, in Reus, and his schooling took place there. However, the family owned a farm in Riudoms, where part of his early life was spent.

Gaudí's family background was far from affluent. His father was a copper smith and boiler maker, and one of his uncles was a wood turner. From an early age he would have been able to absorb the manual skills of a craftsman, developing a feeling for working with materials and learning to respect tools. He attended formal lessons with only moderate success, first at the infant school in Reus, run by Francisco Berenguer, the father of one of his future assistants, and later at the Convent of San Francisco, where he studied for his Bachillerato.

The first indication of an interest in architecture exists in a plan made together with two school friends for the restoration of the Cistercian monastery at Poblet, some twelve miles from Reus. Here the seventeen-year old boy's initiative had been fertilized by the developing nationalist movement in general and, in particular, by the contemporary official restoration of the nearby monastery at Ripoll. While the plans, now preserved in the library at Poblet, show a somewhat ambitious improbability, there is also considerable practical good sense and a care for details regarding costing and provision of water supply. How much official opposition the juvenile efforts would have encountered is impossible to judge, as the trio broke up, and the plan was never pushed forward. Happily, one of the friends, Eduardo Toda, sixty years later was to be instrumental in completing the restoration.

After receiving the coveted Bachillerato in 1869, Gaudí went to Barcelona and enrolled in the Convent of the Carmelites for his pre-university training. Here he took courses in calculus, descriptive geometry, natural history, trigonometry and three-dimensional geometry, acquitting himself well enough in the examinations to gain entrance into the newly established School of Architecture attached to Barcelona University. He studied there from 1873 until 1878. His student days were not free of troubles. Apart from the death of his mother in 1876, there were interruptions to satisfy military service requirements and constant economic pressures from home, obliging him to find work to pay for his education and contribute to the upkeep of the family.

It is not surprising that his concentration on his studies was less than one hundred per cent and in some of his teachers' minds he was far from being a model student, doing his fair share of failing and re-sitting examinations. His extra-curricular paid work as a draftsman was for a number of clients, including the industrial machinery firm, Padrós y Borrás, a rather academic architect, Emilio Sala, the Neo-Gothic architect and teacher at the School of Architecture, Villar, and the master-builder, Fontseré. If these commissions occasionally meant his missing lectures, they did provide him with practical experience, however humble, enabled him to make useful contacts and taught him to budget his time with a scrupulous conscience.

II

Early Projects

Gaudí's final student projects for a fountain, a pier and a university assembly hall show him in earnest heroic mood. The rather pompous style, a mixture of Greek, Neo-Gothic, Romanesque, Baroque and Moorish forms, must inevitably have been the result of the teaching he had received. Already, however, personal qualities had emerged, an urge to fullness, a care for details, an enthusiasm for decorative iron work.

After receiving his degree in 1878 and setting up his private practice, he constructed for himself a rather top-heavy desk, now unfortunately lost. The construction shows little understanding of wood and in parts almost apes the cast iron construction in which his first official commission involved him. This, his only municipal commission ever to be realized, was for the design of street lamps. Understandably, Gaudí was pleased with this early recognition and provided a laboured verbal programme for his design, seeking to inflate its civic importance. The essay is published in full in the Spanish edition of Martinell's study.

Two of the completed lamps now stand in the Plaza Real and a further two, somewhat modified, are in the Plaza del Palacio. The six branching arms, intended to be painted red with gold fluting, hold opaque white shades capped with blue glass domes. The base is decorated with the heraldic shield of the city and the top crowned with the winged helmet of Mercury, symbolic of Barcelona's maritime and commercial interests. Today some of the polychromy can still be seen, but, in general, the robust chunky forms dominate and fit well in the heavy, rather sullen Plaza Real, for which, however, they were not specifically designed.

Desk, now lost, which Gaudí made for himself after his graduation

Lamp post (1879), Plaza Real, Barcelona

(opposite top)
Student project for a pier (1876). School of Architecture, Barcelona

(opposite bottom)
Student project for a university auditorium. School of Architecture, Barcelona

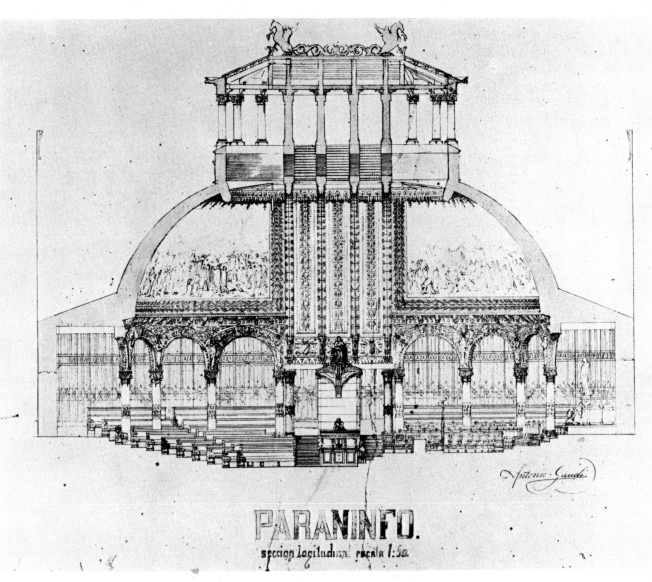

PARANINFO.

seccion Lojitudinal escala 1:50.

13

The Citadel Park, Barcelona (1875-81?)

Before leaving university, Gaudí had worked for the master-builder Fontseré in the creation of the Citadel Park (Parc de La Ciudadela) begun in 1871. He certainly contributed to the calculations for a large iron water tank to service the park, and his project was accepted by the School of Architecture in place of an examination for the course on resistance of materials. There has always been doubt as to any other projects on which he may have collaborated. Certainly, established professionals would very likely have been reluctant to allow whatever work he did much recognition.

The most dominant feature of the park complex was the cascade. The architectural concept of this had nothing to do with Gaudí and was based on a similar fountain at the Palais de Longchamps in Marseilles. Most of the sculpture on the cascade is openly signed by respected sculptors of the day, Nobas, Gamot, Fotats Fluxa. The four splendid winged dragons at the front are, however, unsigned and may well have been Gaudí's invention, together with the two roundels featuring lizards or salamanders on the back wall of the upper terrace. Recent investigation has revealed Gaudí's signature hidden from view on the back of some of the less important figure sculpture.

A photograph exists showing Gaudí in the Punti iron workshops which were responsible for casting the park's boundary railings around 1877. This, together with stylistic evidence based on drawings of decorative iron details for the university hall project, preserved in the

Fountain (c. 1860), Palais de Longchamps, Marseilles, by Espérandieu, with a sculptural group by Pierre-Jules Cavelier

The Citadel Park, monumental fountain

archives of the School of Architecture, suggest Gaudí's involvement in the railings also. Finally, the monument to Aribau, the Catalan economist and man of letters, erected in 1885, has an elaborate stone balustrade surrounding it, which stylistically relates to the outside railings, including the use of the hooded lion's head motive, seen at the base of the park railings. Gaudí's responsibility for this work, however, must remain questionable.

In the Paris International Exhibition of 1878, Gaudí exhibited, along with a design for the shop window of a glove manufacturer, plans for a textile cooperative at Mataró, thirty-five kilometres from Barcelona. This group, inspired by the socialism of Fourier, had been founded in 1865 to protect workers' interests and organize relief during strikes. Gaudí knew the manager of the cooperative, Salvador Pagés, and in a spirit of youthful idealism worked for the organization from 1878 until 1884 alongside his friend from university days, Emilio Cabañas.

Some thirty workers' houses were projected in a symmetrical modular plan, together with a machine shop and social clubhouse. The foundation stone was laid in 1874. The three-storey clubhouse with provision for meeting rooms, billiards room, gymnasium, library and warehouse space was never built. The façade shows an unadventurous scholastic exercise, comparable with the late student projects, and the only point of interest is the incongruously attached spiral staircase linking the garden to the main floor.

The machine shop was built and still exists as part of a private factory. The arches, supporting a flat tile roof, are made of slats of laminated wood bolted together. They span the twelve-metre width of the room and provide what appears to be the first structural use of the parabola. However, as Martinell has pointed out, the outer edges of these arches carry no stress and could just as well be straight.

The Mataró Cooperative, machine shop

The Citadel Park, monumental fountain, a dragon

The Vicens House, Barcelona (1883-85)

In 1878 Barcelona entered a period of investment which lasted until a bank crisis in 1882. It was perhaps this spirit of economic optimism which inspired Vicens, a ceramic and tile manufacturer, to commission a suburban villa. Gaudí's earliest designs date from 1878, but construction did not take place until 1883-85, by which time the economic climate had changed. The house, now almost twice its original size due to alterations made by the subsequent owner, swanks rather immodestly on the sloping Calle Carolinas. The original garden has been reduced owing to a later widening of the street, and a garden fountain incorporating a decorative parabolic arch in brick was destroyed c. 1946. The first impression is of ostentation and indulgence. It is difficult to decide whether this is to be explained as nouveau riche taste wearing its affluence in public or as youthful bravado on the part of Gaudí, thirty-one years old, but embarking on his first major private commission.

The richly fretted façade of rubble stone and pink brick is bridled with floral ceramic girdles. The site was not large, and Gaudí chose to emphasize height by making the verticals of the chimneys carry down the façade and by using a jagged roof silhouette emphasized by turrets. Toothed and stepped brick courses seem to hang from the top of the building like some geometric falling creeper. The lines of the building are sharp, well defined and non-organic. The dynamism of the façade is one of strapping, weaving, cutting back and over-playing. A small projecting balcony at the side, now glazed, was originally open and fitted with Japanese wooden blinds. It contained a small pedestal fountain elaborately fitted with an up-right circular metal web, over which the water splayed. Water and sun, caught together in the web, created a rainbow spectrum.

The most famous detail of this house is the spiky wrought- and cast-iron railing. The repeated palm frond modules were constructed from a drawing by Gaudí's helper, Berenguer. It shows a new confidence, lacking in the more traditional iron window grilles, and was nicely echoed in the real palms growing in the garden and in the painted palms in the small domes of the balcony. Inside, the richness is continued, but there is little originality in

The Vicens House

(above)
The Vicens House, detail of the façade

(right)
The Vicens House, door to the 'fumoir'

The Vicens House, detail of the dining room ceiling　　　　*The Vicens House, the Moorish 'fumoir'*

planning. Gaudí was still ruled by symmetry in the whole and in the organization of individual rooms. Inventiveness and joyful enthusiasm are, however, very much in evidence in the elaborately carved and moulded surfaces. Similar to the 'hortus conclusus' effect of a William Morris wallpaper, Gaudí converted the dining room into an artificial aviary and greenhouse. There are painted panels of flying birds and pink and red carnations painted on small corbels near the ceiling, which itself is divided by wooden beams and the intervals clustered with berries, fruits and leaves in coloured plaster.

There is access from this dining room to the small 'fumoir', only twelve feet wide, its walls lined with ceramic and heavily embossed papier mâché tiles. The low honeycombed ceiling is Gaudí's most obvious quote from the Moorish style, and from it hangs a glass lantern decorated with blue Arabic writing.

'El Capricho', Comillas (1883-85)

While the Casa Vicens was being constructed, Cristobal Cascante, a former university colleague, was supervising the realization of Gaudí's plans for a house at Comillas in northern Spain. Known as 'El Capricho', this house was commissioned by a wealthy tycoon Máximo Diaz de Quijano.

Settled into steeply rising ground, the building consists of a heavy long rectangle modified by shallow round-cornered bays. A coach house is attached to one end, at the other is the main entrance capriciously placed to cut across the corner. Here, above a small porch of four squat columns, a cylindrical tower rises carrying a small cupola on twisted iron columns. The cylindrical form, already used in the student project for a pier, contains Gaudí's first use of the spiral snail staircase. The main block has a rusticated stone base, above which the thin yellow brick-work is banded with six-inch square tiles embossed with yellow and brown sunflowers. These, together with plain lustre green tiles, cover the tower and provide a framed emphasis to the windows. A small sample of the sunflower tiles was used on the balcony of the Casa Vicens. The colour scheme contrasts strongly with the pink stonework of the nearby Neo-Gothic palace and mausoleum chapel

(opposite)
'El Capricho'

19

for Antonio Lopez y Lopez, first marqués de Comillas built by Martorell. The floral motif is developed in the chimneys and cupola, all suggestive of seed pods, and in the sharp vegetation of the capitals in the porch.

The rounded corners of the main bay are emphasized by being cut back and fitted with low hanging iron balconies, in which slatted seats are ingeniously incorporated. The pulling of iron into berried tendrils for the canopy contrasts well with the lower panels of cast honeycomb pattern.

At the back of the house, a retaining wall and staircase in decorative stepped brickwork, set off with plain white tiles, are still extant. Inside, a hexagonal entrance vestibule leads to the same corridor arrangement of rooms Gaudí had used in the Casa Vicens. One interesting detail involves the use of sash windows. Inside the sash channels were concealed bells which rang when the window was lifted. Gaudí always found time for the wonder of such childlike details.

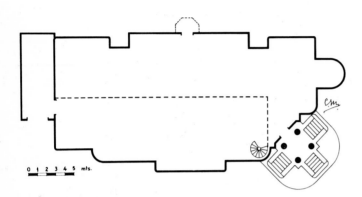

'El Capricho', ground plan

(opposite)
'El Capricho', balcony corner of the front façade

'El Capricho'

The Güell Pavilions, Barcelona (1884-88)

Gaudí's secular patronage was narrow and inbred, coming from first or second generation self-made men who had played a part in Catalonia's recent economic expansion. In 1878 Gaudí, working for the architect Martorell, had produced a wooden Neo-Gothic pew for the chapel of the marqués de Comillas. Both Máximo Diaz de Quijano, the owner of 'El Capricho', and Eusebio Güell, Gaudí's most important patron, were related by marriage to the house of Comillas. Subsequently Güell's patronage, directly or indirectly, was to recommend Gaudí to other textile industrialists, Calvet, Andrés, Batlló and Milá.

Eusebio Güell (1846–1918) in 1878 inherited the fortune and the spinning mills established by his father thirty years earlier. Educated in Spain and France, a student of law, economics and social sciences, he had travelled widely. He saw the cotton industry boom, was responsible for developing corduroy, and, apart from textile interests, was the first industrialist in Spain to establish a Portland cement company, a fact of some small consequence to Gaudí. Ennobled in 1910, the erudite and cosmopolitan Güell proved a generous patron of all the arts and a faithful supporter of Catalan nationalism.

Güell's introduction to Gaudí's work may have been at the Paris International Exhibition of 1878. His first commission was for a hunting lodge. Gaudí provided a drawing but the project was not realized. In 1884, however, the partnership began in real terms with the construction of two pavilions for Güell's estate at Pedralbes on the outskirts of Barcelona. The two single-storey buildings cut across a corner of what is now the modern Avenida de la Victoria. The caretaker's house on the left is octagonal, roofed with a cupola and decorative chimneys reminiscent of those at Comillas. The rectangular stable block on the right is constructed with transverse parabolic arches, a development of those used in the Mataró workshop. Leading off from the stables is a square room with a circular vault, formerly used as a riding school.

The two buildings are connected by the splendid iron dragon gateway five metres wide, a brilliant example of Gaudí's manipulation of iron work in more than the traditional one plane. The dragon itself refers either to the St. George legends or to fairy stories of such guardians of enchanted places. Originally Gaudí incorporated the conceit of making the dragon raise one of its claws when an intruder opened the gate.

This is a concentrated example of Gaudí's rich combinations of materials: two tones of brickwork, one pink, one yellow, set off by the sparkle from fragments of ceramic embedded in the mortar, boldly pressed stucco decoration, stone rubble, coloured tiles and a variety of wrought-, cast- and meshed-iron. The third generation International Style high-rise blocks erected on the opposite side of the road look impoverished by comparison.

One remarkable feature is the use of an 'in-growing'

The Güell Pavilions

The Güell Pavilions, ground plan

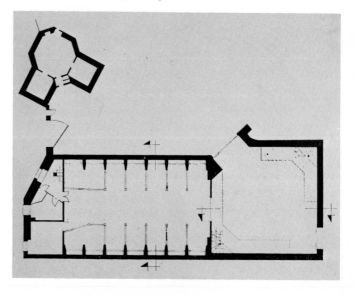

The Güell Pavilions, dome

corner. This treatment had been hinted at in the Casa Vicens and in the balcony corners of 'El Capricho'. It could have been influenced by the illustration of a Gothic corner in Viollet's *Entretiens* and confirmed by such examples as the corner niches on the late Gothic hospital of Santa Cruz.

*   *   *

The Casa Vicens, 'El Capricho' and the Güell Pavilions show Gaudí's early interest in Moorish art, with its patterned brickwork, use of coloured ceramic tiles and overall richness. There is no Arabic art indigenous to Catalonia, but there was certainly a fashionable interest in Moorish forms from the 1870s to the early 1890s, partly inspired by the Moroccan expedition of 1860. In 1875 the municipal authorities in Barcelona proposed a monument to Spanish victories in Africa, one of the prizes going to an Arabian style project which was never realized. On Tibidabo, one of the mountains overlooking Barcelona, however, an observation and rest pavilion was constructed in the Arabic style, and more than one building built in these years introduced Moorish quotations, including

The Güell Pavilions, detail of the dragon gateway

The Güell Pavilions, the dragon gateway

the horse-shoe arch, very directly exploited in the 1892 bullring in the Plaza España.

In his history of architecture course at the university Gaudí would certainly have been introduced to the study of Arabic art. There was no lack of literature on the subject, and the two sumptuous volumes in colour by Owen Jones on the Alhambra decorations (1845, with text in French and English) were available to him in the school library. It is worth speculating that Owen Jones's scrupulous itemizing and translation of all Arabic inscriptions on the Alhambra may have encouraged Gaudí's subsequent interest in developing his own kind of 'speaking buildings'.

In 1887 the Compañia Transatlantica, owned by the marqués de Comillas, was represented at the Naval Exhibition in Cadiz by a pavilion in the Moorish style, actually incorporating plaster casts from the Alhambra. It appears this pavilion, with modifications, was used again the following year at the Barcelona International Exhibition, one of whose directors was the same marqués. Recently discovered documents leave no doubt that Gaudí did play some role in this venture.

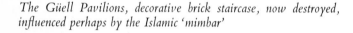
The Güell Pavilions, decorative brick staircase, now destroyed, influenced perhaps by the Islamic 'mimbar'

(opposite)
*The Vicens House, detail of a
corner*

*The Güell Pavilions, detail of
an 'in-growing' corner*

The Güell Palace, Barcelona (1885-90)

The Palau Güell is a stronghold of wealth. With the exception of the entrance gates, the façade is poker-faced. Inside, however, is a virtuoso exhibition of coffered ceilings and carved dados, a blatant expression of assets in terms of ivory, marble, gilded metal, inlaid wood, brocades and stained glass.

The house was built as an extension of Güell's existing town house on 'Las Ramblas'. It faces on to the Calle del Asalto, whose narrowness makes a telling façade impossible.

Reading the six storeys vertically from the entrance vestibule, a spiralling ramp for horses leads down to basement stables with their impressive mushroom columns in brick. Upwards from the entrance a staircase leads to the mezzanine containing waiting rooms, a library and administrative offices. From here there is access to the main floor whose suite of rooms is arranged around a central, square sitting room replacing what in more typical plans would have been a central air patio. This central room rises to the roof and culminates in a deep blue, honeycomb-tiled dome, studded with stars. It contains an organ, a minstrel's gallery and a private chapel concealed behind elaborate segmented doors in ivory and precious woods. The dining room, conveniently placed adjacent to the main room, has access to a garden terrace at the rear of the building. The bedrooms ring the central room on the fifth and sixth floors, the most important having shutters opening on to the magical blue dome (see p.35).

Away from this retreat of affluent gloom, on the roof, the mood changes, and Gaudí introduced his first play space. Fenced in by pseudo-battlements the chimney pots and ventilation shafts, covered in broken ceramic, erupt around a central cone corresponding to the inside dome. This cone, crowned with the bat from the arms of Catalonia, is perforated with openings to allow daylight to shine through the stars of the dome. An electric light bulb is ingeniously placed above each opening for use at night.

Two significant aspects of the building need isolating. The first is Gaudí's manipulation of space, both vertically

(opposite)
The Güell Palace, street façade

The Güell Palace, section

The Güell Palace, parabolic entrance gate

and horizontally; horizontally by the stepping of floor and ceiling levels and vertically by the use of semi-transparent partitions, which may be bannisters, arcades of columns or a lattice of turned wooden spindles. By such screening methods, borrowed from Moorish example, real access, along with light, is filtered through a series of transitional stages. There is the constant invitation to look through and move through.

Secondly, there is the process of orchestrating a single theme; the parabolic arch, for instance, used as a decorative motif, is declared in grandeur in the two entrance gates, expressive of arrival and departure, is then picked up in the lead-grey columns of the main salon, glorified in the arches of the dome, muted and turned upside down in the decorative venetian blind for the rear façade and last seen in the hooded openings of the roof cone.

(opposite)
The Güell Palace, rear façade

The Güell Palace, pinnacle of the cone on the roof

The Güell Palace, detail of the roof chimneys

(above and opposite)
The Güell Palace, interiors

*The Güell Palace, spiral ramp
leading to the stables*

The Convent and School of Santa Teresa, Barcelona (1889-94)

Overlapping with the completion of the Palau Güell, Gaudí's school and convent for the order of Santa Teresa is an excellent example of his ability to change moods. Here an almost puritanical simplicity, a formal and spiritual uprightness, is dominant. The long rectangular block, gripped into compactness by the corner turrets, is modified only by the slight projection of the entrance portico and a bay window at the rear. The first two floors of cheap ochre rubble contrast with the red brick above. On the third floor Gaudí played with the repetition of simple units, stating this obviously in the saw-toothed battlements and developing it more sensitively in the rhythm of triangular window hoods suggestive of elongated parabolas. This rhythm is quickened by introducing intermediary blind arches and is given greater tonal insistence by stepping back the brickwork so that the

(opposite)
The Güell Palace, interior of the dome (see pp. 28–33)

The Convent of Santa Teresa, detail of a corner

The Convent of Santa Teresa, front façade

(opposite left)
The Güell Palace, roof chimney
(see pp. 28–33)

(opposite right)
The Park Güell, detail of the
bench (see pp. 48–51)

(opposite)
The Park Güell, dragon
(see pp. 48–51)

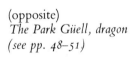

The Convent of Santa Teresa,
detail of the front façade

top of the building appears to be made of cut-away laminations.

The plainness and rigour is continued inside. The plan, largely symmetrical, is a strip arrangement with a central corridor on the long axis, with air wells, giving access to the flanking parallel rooms. On the second floor, Gaudí, with originality, abandoned load-bearing walls and substituted a corridor of white parabolic arches with the effect of producing an interior cloister. These arches, simply plastered, rise from slender columns of exposed red brick, one unit wide, and are supported by the lower floor reinforced with metal beams and brick corbels.

Despite constant demands for economy by the patron, the Reverend Enrique de Ossó, Gaudí did introduce precious touches: in the corner towers which he topped with ceramic crosses and inset with spiralling brick columns, in the entrance portico with the coat of arms of the order set between panels of open decorative brickwork, in the fine iron entrance gate and in the wrought-iron grille for the door cleverly composed of 'S' and 'T' forms.

The Convent of Santa Teresa, interior corridor of the second storey

The Archbishop's Palace, Astorga (1887-93)

In 1886 a fire destroyed the episcopal residence in Astorga and in the following year Bishop Grau, a native of Reus, commissioned a new building from Gaudí. Such a public commission came under the jurisdiction of central academic authorities in Madrid, and Gaudí, prevented from working as he liked, had to submit detailed plans and be willing to make compromises.

Construction began in 1889, yet Gaudí himself did not visit the site until 1890, when he took with him a body of Catalan craftsmen to the annoyance of the locals. In 1893 Bishop Grau died, and Gaudí, finding himself at odds with parochial bureaucracy, resigned, leaving what is perhaps his most unhappy commission half complete. In 1907 a young architect, Luís de Guereta, finally roofed the building, paying little respect to Gaudí's original provision of a central light patio and a high pyramidal silhouette for the roof.

The palace in white granite is basically square with cylindrical corner towers. The interior is symmetrically planned around a central hall. A chapel and a throne room, both two storeys high, are placed at the two ends of the main axis. Perhaps the most personal feature of the building is the entrance portico with its interconnecting, obliquely hooded arches.

Although the project had caused much frustration and an ultimate abortion, it had been useful to Gaudí for the contact with the bishop himself, who is thought to have been a fundamental influence on Gaudí's spiritual development in these years.

The Archbishop's Palace, Astorga

The House of 'Los Botines', León (1891-94)

Gaudí was introduced by Güell to the textile and banking firm of Fernandez y Andrés in León, and in late 1891 he began a five-storey house for this new patron, including warehouse and apartment space. The name of the building is derived partly from a pun on the name of the first owner of the firm, Homs y Botinás, and partly from the Spanish word for booty, *botin*, since some pots of money were found on the site during preliminary excavations.

With a prestigious position in the town centre, the house presents a compact rough granite block, capped at the corners with round towers terminating at first floor level. There is no absence of Gothic prototypes for this feature. The curiously unfinished corner towers, known as Bartizans, on the Archivo de La Corona de Aragón in the Plaza del Rey near Barcelona Cathedral, may well have been in Gaudí's mind.

Gaudí asserted his own loyalties and the Catalan business connections of the firm by placing a sculpture of St. George and the dragon above the main door, St. George being the patron saint of Catalonia. He showed pragmatic commonsense by providing the basement storage floor with a dry moat to allow for light and air and by building the working areas with non-load bearing walls, substituting a more flexible plan of iron stanchions and beams which anticipate the use of such a system later in the Casa Milá.

(right)
The House of 'Los Botines'

The House of 'Los Botines', St. George and the dragon sculpture above the entrance

The Tangiers Project (1892)

In 1887 Gaudí had accompanied Claudio, second marqués de Comillas, on a diplomatic visit to Morocco. In connection with this rare trip away from Barcelona, he was engaged in 1892 on a project for a Franciscan mission in Tangiers. The project, although ostensibly for a religious order, was not without economic and political significance. However, it was never realized, and the drawings were lost in 1936. The project is known from a single existing photograph dedicated to Andrés, his patron in León, and kept in the archives of the School of Architecture in Barcelona. The building, set in a quatrefoil enclosure, anticipates the Sagrada Familia in its exuberant play with vertical towers. Significantly Gaudí is known to have kept a drawing of this project on the wall of his office on the Sagrada Familia site.

(opposite)
The Calvet House, front façade

The Tangiers Project, a photograph preserved at the School of Architecture, Barcelona

The Calvet House, Barcelona (1898-1904)

After his withdrawal from Astorga and the completion of 'Los Botines', there is a mysterious four-year gap, from 1894 to 1898, of comparatively little activity in Gaudí's career. A breathing space in his career, it may well have been the time when the forty-two year old architect took stock of his achievement to date and redirected his energies in terms of his increasingly zealous commitment to religion.

The Casa Calvet, commissioned by the textile manufacturer Pedro Martin Calvet, is Gaudí's most conservative building and was awarded a prize in 1900 by the municipal authorities. The narrow five-storey façade is in a rather tightly disciplined Baroque style. The fenestration is regular, with five rectangular windows to each floor, the second and fourth being emphasized with convex balconies. The brackets supporting these balconies and the bay window unit above the central entrance are decorated with realistic carvings of fruit and berries, a minor form of Grinling Gibbons in stone.

The symmetry of the exterior is continued in the simple axial planning of the interior. A central open lift shaft is flanked by two smaller light-wells, all topped with glass skylights. In the entrance vestibule the lift itself is a focus

of interest. This modern piece of machinery has been treated with ironic reverence. Converted into an elaborate reliquary casket in carved wood with decorative iron work, it is surrounded with a baldacchino of twisted columns in polished artificial granite which continue through the full height of the building (see p. 71).

(see p. 71)

The staircase wrapping around the lift shaft is decorated with painted bunches of grapes, the walls half covered in bright Delft blue tiles, their whirling floral motif echoing the overlapping circles of twisted wrought-iron of the banister railings. The wooden handrails, sinuous and highly polished, are drawn into a knob-like berry when they meet the corner granite columns, a form which Gaudí had used in the metal work for 'El Capricho'.

(right)
The Calvet House, door-knocker. The caller is invited to squash the malicious beetle with the Christian crosses.

(bottom right)
The Calvet House, chair

The Calvet House, bay window

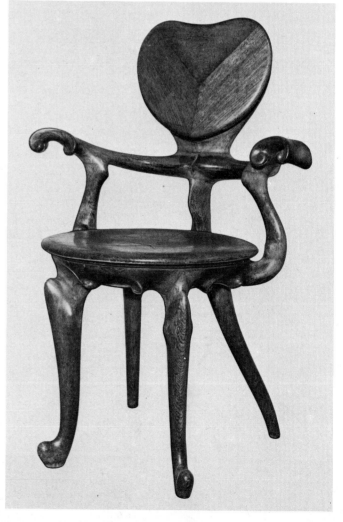

'Bellesguard', Barcelona (1900–02)

This 'Beautiful Spot', high on the slopes of Tibidabo, was the site of the early fifteenth-century castle of Martin I, the last King of Catalonia. The upright fortressed aspect of this house preserves the memory of its heritage. It was commissioned by Dona Maria Sagués.

The house exhibits a separation of simple geometrical elements, rare in Gaudí's work, the square bell tower cutting cleanly into one corner, the arcade of windows preserved in the same kind of long rectangle favoured by Gaudí's contemporary, Puig i Cadafalch, and, perhaps the most interesting feature, the steep roof, a truncated

'Bellesguard'

pyramid pierced by the angled projections of dormer windows. This roof is routed for exploration with a delightful stepped path, and its sliced facets recall the treatment of Güell's hunting lodge at Garraf (1888–90), built by Berenguer with Gaudí's overseeing. The façade is covered in a blue-green, slate-like stone, set off by the knobbled stone work around the entrance and by later decorative iron grilles and panels of ceramic, the work of a young assistant, Sugrañes.

Inside, the top floor room, the most interesting, is a brilliant example of Catalan bricklaying skills. Here, load bearing walls are replaced by a central row of brick columns, the courses progressively cantilevered out to form capitals which continue into a brick beam. From this beam a fanned system of arches rises to support a flat Catalan tile ceiling.

In constructing this house, certain modifications were made to the surrounding land, involving the building of a retaining wall to support the servicing road. Here Gaudí experimented with clumsy inclined piers which anticipate their more sophisticated use in the Park Güell.

(opposite)
'Bellesguard', detail of the roof

(right)
'Bellesguard', interior of a top-storey room

'Bellesguard', stepped path on the roof

46

The Park Güell, Barcelona (1900-14)

Around 1900 Güell had the idea of developing a garden
suburb on the 'Montana Pelada', which as its name implied
was a barren, literally 'bald', hill on the outskirts of
Barcelona. It was to have been rather like a miniature
version of the English Bedford Park, purely residential
and, unlike Ebenezer Howard's idea of a garden city,
without any industrial buildings. The colony, extending
the small estate and house Güell already owned, was some
thirty-eight acres and was to have contained sixty housing
plots. It would have been mildly cooperative, sharing such
services as water, lighting and transport. The only
restriction on purchasers of land was that they should not
build on more than one-sixth of the individual plots and
that the remaining garden spaces were to be bounded by
walls no more than forty centimetres high.

As a housing experiment it was a total failure. Only two
houses were built, one, the original show house, built by
Berenguer, was lived in by Gaudí himself from 1906 to
1926, and the second was lived in by a friend Dr. Alfonso
Trias. Presumably the middle classes for whom the project

(right)
The Park Güell, gatehouses

*The Park Güell, iron fence designed for the Vicens House but now
in the Park Güell*

was intended were not only resistant to estate living, but also understandably cautious of moving to such an unfashionable area so far from the centre of the city. Converted into a municipal park, however, it is brilliantly successful and constitutes the finest example of Gaudí's sensitive collaboration with nature.

Encroached upon now by the subsequent conurbation, the park is approached through steeply rising streets. An eeling boundary wall is reached, decorated with circular ceramic nameplates. The main entrance is flanked by two small buildings housing the gatekeeper and providing waiting rooms and lavatory and telephone services. Both have elaborate ceramic-coated roofs, and the house at the left is distinguished for its twisting spire topped with a cross and supported on twisted metal columns, first seen in the 'El Capricho' tower. It is worth noting that this spire is one of the first examples in Spain of reinforced concrete construction. The original gates were wooden and have since been replaced by iron fencing taken from the Casa Vicens.

A double flight of steps with ceramic bannisters rises from the entrance, and at the right of this is a small

(left)
The Park Güell, Doric columns for the market hall

The Park Güell, double staircase

The Park Güell, arcade

(opposite top)
The Park Güell, ceramic bench enclosing a theatre/play arena

(opposite bottom)
The Park Güell, detail of the ceiling of the market hall

The Park Güell, plan

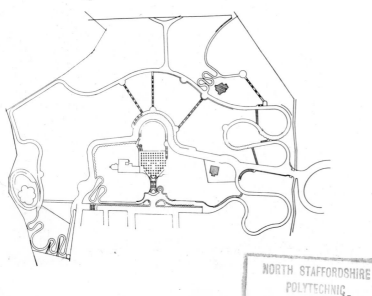

circular coach shed, its large mushrooming central stone column previewed in the basement brick columns of the Palau Güell. Ascending the stairs, various ceramic decorations are passed until a recessed market hall is reached. Developed from a natural concavity in the hill, this covered space is colonnaded with idiosyncratic Doric columns. The columns, six metres high and made of artificial stone, are fluted, have white ceramic leggings and are given an emphasized inward lean. They also have a hollow central core for drainage. Water is conducted through them to a cistern at the back of the hall, where it would have been stored for the community's use. The roof is divided into a network of squares, each with a shallow cupped dome covered in broken ceramic and glass mosaic.

Side stairs lead to the open air arena and terrace above the market hall. Originally intended for theatrical events, the children of Barcelona now find it a very adequate, if dusty, football pitch. The notable feature of this esplanade is the snaking ceramic bench which edges it. One of Gaudí's happiest ideas, it is thought to have begun with a workman being asked to strip off and sit on a bed of plaster and finished with Gaudí's assistant Jujol meticulously breaking and jigsawing the ceramic coating over the warped surfaces.

The remaining part of the park, as the graceful plan shows, is rippled with paths, expressive of natural contours; their sinuous bends provide a constant invitation of corners and the joys of surprise. The main routes are carried on four stretches of arcades and viaducts supported by tilted columns, each treated differently in the detailing of the columns and the nature of the vaulting. Grotto-like in appearance, these arcades provide shelter from sun and rain. The highest spot was to have been reserved for a chapel in the shape of a rose. Unfortunately, only a small spiralling mound with three stone crosses today hints at this intention. From here the whole park can be seen as a natural acropolis 150 metres above the sea, offering splendid views over Barcelona.

The Batlló House, Barcelona (1904-06)

Commissioned by the textile manufacturer, José Batlló y Casanovas, Gaudí gave a rather ordinary house, built on the elegant Paseo de Gracia in 1875–77, a total face-lift. He added a fifth floor for servants' quarters, provided a new and varied reorganization of room spaces on the main floor and remodelled the façade so that it could compete with its next door neighbour, the Casa Amatller of 1900 by Puig i Cadafalch.

The narrow, smokey blue-grey façade has become jewellery on a large scale. Gaudí clasped around the existing structure what amount to very elaborate architectural spectacles, setting the windows of the first floor deeply in egg-shaped stone frames and dividing them with slender knuckled columns which give a feeling of brittle elegance. The upper wall is coated in a blue and green ceramic cosmetic, studded with disks, which caused Dali to talk of 'the tranquil waters of a lake', but which today has lost much of its 'shining iridescence'.

The roof is perhaps the most fanciful invention, covered in scale-like tiles and contoured with a writhing backbone, notched with blue and brown pot-bellies. It provides the story-line for the building seen as an analogue of St. George's dragon.

The central airwell and staircase, covered in pale grey-blue tiles becoming bright blue on the upper floors, has shoulder-high glass screen partitions which allow for maximum light. The covering glass skylight is constructed with metal 'I' beams bent into parabolic arches. A

The Batlló House (in the centre), *front façade, with its neighbour, Puig i Cadafalch's Amatller House*

(opposite)
The Batlló House, staircase

The Batlló House, roof

(right)
The Batlló House, detail of the roof

(opposite left)
The Batlló House, detail of the façade

(opposite right)
The Batlló House, detail of the roof

(opposite)
'Bellesguard', window (see pp. 45–47)

separate staircase with carved and polished wooden hand rails leads to the principal floor, which Gaudí completely reorganized and where he developed for the first time rounded rhythms of the kind Guimard in France had used in the 1902 plans for the Hôtel de Nozal. The suite of rooms comprising waiting rooms, living room, dining room and private chapel is Gaudí's finest group of interiors. Wood and glass screens allow for greater spacial flexibility. The whipped plaster ceiling, executed by Jujol and swirling to a central light fixture, is a splendid invention, and Gaudí's robust furniture, like its author, awkward and contorted in isolation, is especially effective when seen in context.

(opposite top)
The Batlló House, interior

(opposite bottom)
The Batlló House, skylight with 'I' beams bent into parabolic arches

(right)
The Batlló House, double hinged doors for the interior

The Batlló House, glass screen partitions

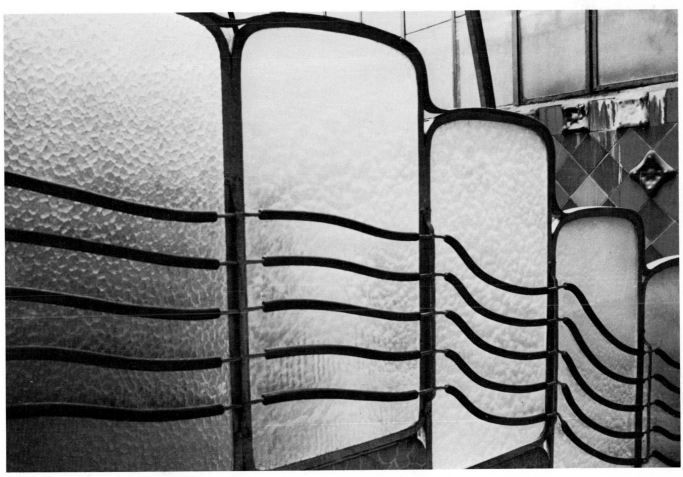

The Milá House, Barcelona (1906-10)

The Casa Milá lumbers impressively around its commanding corner site at the intersection of the Paseo de Gracia and the Calle de Provenza. Built for Batlló's partner, Don Pedro Milá, it is an apartment building of six storeys arranged around two connected courtyards, one circular, the other oval. Originally there was to have been a single central patio with a double spiralling ramp for motorized access to the flats. Limited space prevented this plan from being realized, ramps only being used, as in the Palau Güell, to lead to the basement stables.

From the plan submitted by Gaudí to the municipal authorities in February 1906, it can be seen that certain modifications were made to the façade. The spiralling tower surmounted with a cross which would have emphasized the turn of the corner at the left and the notched vertebrae skyline were dispensed with, as was the gilded bronze statue of the Virgin and Child intended at one stage to be a central decorative and symbolic feature. It is not known whether this was rejected for political expediency or for reasons of the patron's personal taste. The only vestige of such religious commitment is the

Caricature of the Milá House from L'Esquella de la Torratxa

The Milá House

(opposite)
The Milá House, detail of the façade

inscription, 'Ave [Maria] Gratia Dominus Tecum', echoing similar invocations on the Casa Calvet and 'Bellesguard'.

The massive façade in stone from Vilafranca, now more ponderous as it has darkened, is roughly but evenly abraded to catch the light. One elephantine strut obtrudes on to the pavement and somehow was gracefully allowed to comply with municipal building regulations. Decorative iron grilles have been removed from the basement windows to make way for modern shop fronts, but the balconies above are intact. Twisting and slithering like iron flotsam, they still betray signs of original painting.

It is important to emphasize that the whole of this façade, although expressive of the structure concealed behind, is completely separate from it, like the façade of a Gothic cathedral. The building is supported on a free system of pillars in brick and stone in combination with trussed iron girders and beams, and the façade is simply attached by metal tie rods. The flexibility originally desired by Gaudí was astonishing, as the ground plans make clear with their conglomerates of rounded molecular room spaces, actually advertised in the decorative iron

(opposite)
The Milá House, detail of the balconies

(left)
The Milá House, detail of the roof

The Milá House, roof

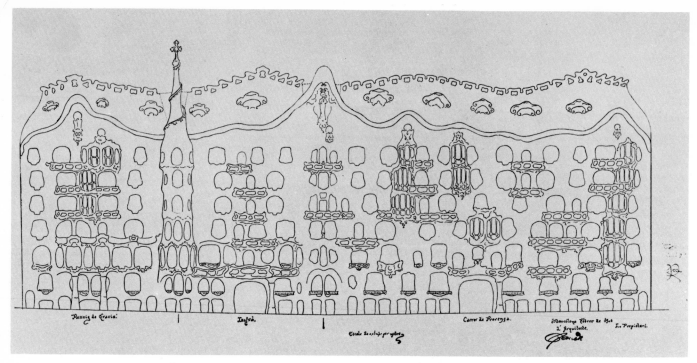

The Milá House, elevation plan submitted to the Barcelona municipal authorities (1906)

The Milá House, original floor plan of the third storey

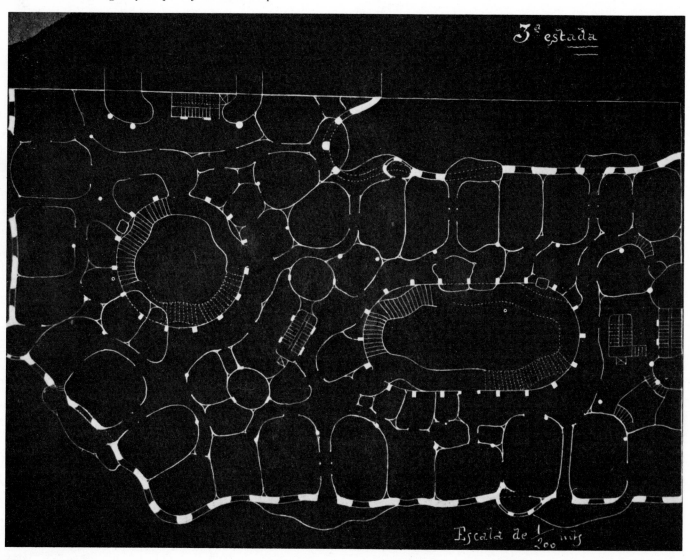

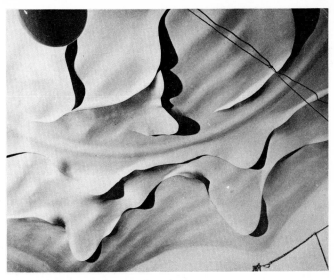

The Milá House, plaster ceiling decoration

(left)
The Milá House, decorative iron door for the main entrance

Hexagonal concrete relief tiles, designed for the Milá House, but
now covering the pavements of the Paseo de Gracia

entrance gates. As built, however, the rooms became more like rectangular polygons.

Returning to the impact of the façade, the paradox of achieving such a fluid modelled form by actually carving huge blocks of stone is continued in the emotional resonance of the building. Seen as a petrified wave or a liquified mountain, it provides the spectator with the kind of associative hybrid which endeared Gaudí to Dali and the Surrealists. The obvious stoneness and cliff-like rearing up has earned it the nickname 'La Pedrera' or 'the quarry', but equally dominant are the sea references, from the undulating roll of the individual floors to the seaweed strappings of the balconies, from the tide marks in Jujol's plaster ceilings to the hexagonal, blue-green tiles incorporating starfish shapes, which Gaudí designed especially for the building and which now cover the pavements of the Paseo de Gracia.

One of the most delightful of all Gaudian experiences is the open roof of this building, adumbrated at the Palau Güell but here treated with fresh exuberance. Carried on a rib-like structure of parabolic arches found in the top storey, the roof is a switchback of hyperbolic shapes, planted with decorative chimneys and ventilation stacks. Even when viewed through washing lines and television aerials, their sentry-like mystery barely disguises a mischievous sense of fun, pawns in the spectator's game of sculptural dodgems.

The Milá House, parabolic brick arches on the top storey

The American Hotel, New York (1908-09)

Around 1908 Gaudí was approached by an American business man who commissioned a design for a hotel in New York, to include exhibition space, lecture halls and restaurants. Matamala, Gaudí's collaborator in sculpture, has provided drawings of this project which show a somewhat ludicrous building still reminiscent of the recent Casa Milá in its lower details. Intended to be only slightly smaller than the Eiffel Tower, the soft-nosed, bullet forms sluggishly torpedo into space. Double exterior walls were to have provided space for lifts and staircases, and a starred spherical observatory space would have finished the design at the top.

Project for a hotel in New York, drawing by Matamala

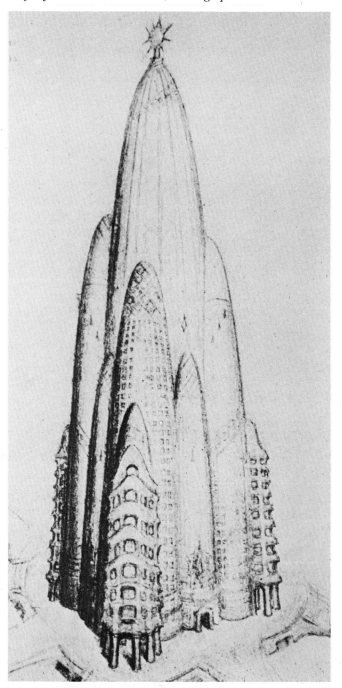

The Infant School for the Sagrada Familia, Barcelona (1909)

This was a cheap simple building erected quickly in 1909 on the site of the future Gloria façade of the Sagrada Familia. Intended, therefore, as a temporary building, it is, nevertheless, still standing today. Resting on a stone base, the rippling brick walls provide an effective counterpoint of convex and concave movements, and the treatment of the tile roof is Gaudí's clearest example of hyperbolic forms. It was a drawing of this building which Le Corbusier chose to record in his notebook during his visit to Barcelona in 1928.

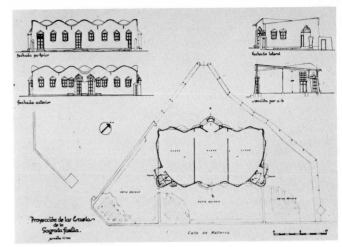

The Infant School for the Sagrada Familia, ground plan and elevations

The Infant School for the Sagrada Familia

The Church at Santa Coloma (1898; 1908-14)

Take a person into a low, far stretching crypt, arched upon numerous short and massive pillars; although he can walk erect and breathe with ease, he will incline his head and none but melancholy thoughts and gloomy images will present themselves to his mind . . . . But, take him into a building vaulted at a lofty height and flooded with light and air. He will direct his gaze upwards and his face will reflect the feelings of grandeur which crowd into his mind.

Viollet-le-Duc, *Entretiens,* Lecture I

The Church at Santa Coloma, drawing made from photographs of the model

This quotation provides a suitable description of Gaudí's project for the Church at Santa Coloma, from darkness to light, from sorrow at Christ's death to joy at his resurrection. In 1891 Güell, perhaps encouraged by his firm's success at the 1889 Paris Exposition Universelle, decided to expand and transplant his father's original textile factory to a new site at Santa Coloma, nine miles west of Barcelona. Mindful of industrial unrest, as a benevolent paternalist, he envisaged some 150 houses for employees serviced by shops, a social club and a church. This small complex was built during the 1890s by Gaudí's young associate, Berenguer, and others. Gaudí himself was commissioned to build the church in 1898. However, construction did not begin until 1908, and during the intervening period he worked alongside the engineer Eduardo Goetz and the sculptor Bertran on the large wire and canvas model, unfortunately now destroyed. In 1915 the crypt was consecrated to the Holy Heart, and with the death of Güell three years later the project was abandoned incomplete. What might have been can be judged from the drawings made from photographs of the model. From the low grounded crypt the elevated space of the main church would have risen with its parabolic spires and ample window spaces, a place of height and light.

Ten years of preparation may seem extensive, but it must be remembered these years were professionally very busy and crowded with other projects (see Chronology p. 90); also the preparatory model was the most thorough calculation of a catenary system. This system consists of determining by experiment the forces of tension acting on a structure by attaching to a wire model small calculated weights. The structure is then inverted and the resulting tension forces converted into forces of compression. Such a procedure was not only highly complex, but also without modern precedent. Giovanni Poleni, an Italian theorist and mathematician, discussed such a system in 1748, but it is unlikely that Gaudí knew of this. More pertinent is the reference found by Prof. Bassegoda to the catenary in John Millington's *Elements of Architecture,* published in Philadelphia in 1839, the Spanish translation of 1848 being available in the library of the School of Architecture.

Crouching half-way up a low hill is the finished crypt. Approached from a narrow street of terraced yellow brick houses, it seems to have bedded itself comfortably into the uneven ground and is surrounded, almost camou-

The Church at Santa Coloma, model

(above)
The Church at Santa Coloma, crypt

(below)
The Church at Santa Coloma, hooded windows

flaged, by a copse of pine trees. To the right, a stepped ramp brings a helter-skelter movement, which would have spiralled upwards throughout the whole façade, but today succeeds only in arriving at the aborted entrance posts of the upper church. The first section of this ramp acts as the roof for a sunken, bench-lined waiting area. The second section, supported by slanting columns, provides a canopy for the crypt's portico, vaulted with decorative hyperbolic paraboloids and studded with triangular orange stones and ceramic crosses. Passing through this transitional shaded space, the inside of the crypt is dark, despite the stained glass windows with their petalled crosses in blue, yellow and pink. The semi-elliptical space is divided into two levels, firstly, the main body of the crypt, its scalloped edges echoing the 'Tridacna' clam shells placed at the entrance as holy water stoups. Secondly, behind an undulating humped wall, there is a small raised gallery, arcaded with six columns chequered half brick, half dark cement.

Despite initial confusion regarding the pillars of the main space, the arrangement resolves itself into the following system: four central inclined pillars in grey basalt stone, each one made up of five sections, primitively hacked, and 'cemented' with lead. They are prefaced by the single stone column in the porch, about whose symbolic significance Loyer has aptly remarked 'Tu es Pierre et sur cette pierre Je bâtirai mon église.' Around this central baldacchino are ringed ten circular columns in pink brick all without capitals; four of these are especially massive, fully clad in grey cement while the remainder have cement footings. Two large columns flank the arcaded gallery, two slanting columns frame a shallow chapel on the left, housing a crucifix, and two more straddle a spiralling cylindrical element on the right, which contains the rope for the small outside bell tower. All the columns are smoothed into the floor without distinctive base mouldings. With the smell of pines in the air, it is not difficult to be reminded of tree bark in Gaudí's treatment of some of the surfaces of these columns.

The roofing of the crypt, previewed at 'Bellesguard', is flat, made of red terracotta tiles, articulated in the centre by two fans of ribs and carried on triangular brick partitions which splay outwards. There is a second system of arches joining the outer walls to the first circle of columns. The complexity of the result is justified rather for its decorative palm-like effect than for structural economy, although the load of the intended upper church must be remembered. Just as the play with various levels helps the building to accommodate itself to the lie of the land, reminiscent of the vine terraces stepping the hills near Tarragona, so too the colour of the building is equally collaborative with nature. Dry sandy rubble and pale pink brick for the main walls are dampened by the

The Church at Santa Coloma, interior of the crypt showing Gaudí's specially designed seats

use of greenish-grey schist and black cinder-stones for the ramp and heightened by restrained touches of colour, such as the reveals of the hooded windows covered in broken ceramic mosaic. This primitive shelter for the faithful, so self-consciously rough, is paradoxically Gaudí's most neat and elegant work.

(opposite)
The Calvet House, staircase with the lift (see pp. 42–44)

(left)
The Church at Santa Coloma, portico of the crypt

(bottom left)
The Church at Santa Coloma, crypt. 'Tridacna' shell forms are used as holy water stoups. Notice the absence of base mouldings to the pier.

The Church at Santa Coloma, plan of the crypt

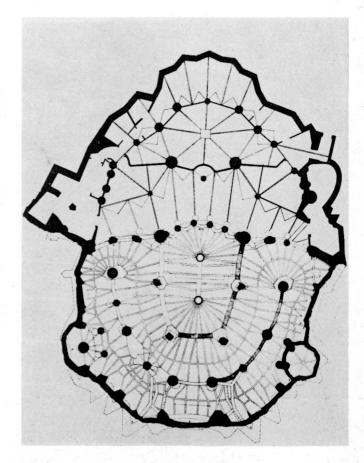

The Sagrada Familia, Barcelona (1883-1926)

In 1866 Bocabella, a bookseller in Barcelona, established the spiritual association of St. Joseph. This cult, parented by Joseph Huguet in Dijon, was supported by Pius IX, who in 1870 declared St. Joseph a Patron of the Universal Church. In 1874, Bocabella opened a public subscription account with the purpose of building a church, the Sagrada Familia, for the association, and by 1881 enough contributions had been received for the purchase of a five-acre plot of land in the Barrio del Poblet. This was a poor district on the outskirts of Barcelona where country people were being slowly and often painfully urbanized. The building was commissioned from the respected architect Villar, who drew up an unadventurous plan, and the foundation stone was laid in 1882. Perhaps Villar was disturbed by the insecurity of being financed by public subscriptions or felt that there were more prestigious demands on his talents; whatever the reason, he soon resigned. Martorell, the official assessor of the church, took over for a short time and then recommended the appointment of Gaudí. In 1883, therefore, when excavations for the crypt had just been completed, the thirty-one year old Gaudí began his association with this project, precisely at the same time as he was building the Casa Vicens.

(opposite)
The Sagrada Familia, Portal of the Passion with the Portal of the Nativity behind

The Sagrada Familia, ground plan

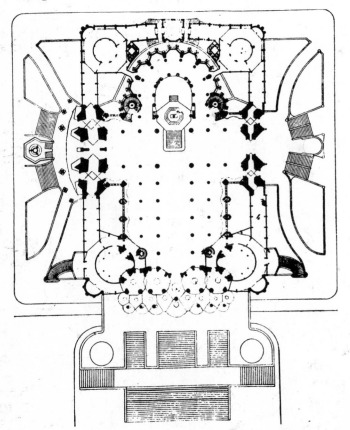

Gaudí finished vaulting the crypt by 1887, making some modifications to Villar's original plan, and work went ahead on the apse, which by 1893 had reached fifty metres. At this point, Bocabella having died the previous year, the Bishop of Barcelona intervened and made official what had formerly been a private venture, by setting up a commission which ratified Gaudí's appointment. The east façade was begun, and despite other secular commissions resulting in Gaudí's constant absenteeism, its three portals had been erected by 1901. Activity went ahead in fits and starts, dependent on money and Gaudí's commitments. In 1914, however, the sixty-two year old architect, in retreat from the world, decided to spend all his time on the church in a spirit of obsessive sacrifice, which resulted in his living on the site. He took such a personal interest in the raising of money that, it is said, people would cross to the other side of the street when they saw him coming.

Certainly Gaudí never intended the work to be finished in his lifetime. Like the medieval cathedrals, it was to be a work of generations; 'My client is in no rush' he is reported to have said. When he died in 1926 work continued under a group of close collaborators, Sugrañes, Quintana, Matamala, people who could be relied upon to translate the master's ideas most faithfully.

In 1935 work halted at the outbreak of the Spanish Civil War, during which, fire gutted part of the building, and the models and plans in Gaudí's studio were destroyed. Dalí in his *Intimate Biography* bizarrely records that 'An old friend of the architect . . . claims to have seen the unearthed body of the architect of genius dragged through the streets of Barcelona by a rope that children had fastened around his neck.'

Following this sacrilege little could be done until a new model had been constructed. After the centenary celebrations of Gaudí's birth in 1952 a further spurt of building took place, still relying on public subscriptions. Today work continues slowly with the architectural world in division as to its advisability. Many believe that with a new generation of workers, unacquainted directly with Gaudí's spirit, it is impossible to do justice to the original vision. Others feel this does not matter and think the project, rather than being kept to some kind of facsimile of what Gaudí might have done, ought to be widened out to include modern initiative. Even more radical is the call for a reformulation of the problem, not how to finish the work, but, accepting that it can never be finished, how to use what now exists.

Gaudí's Plan

A focus for the long straight roads constructed as part of the new grid system development of Barcelona, the Sagrada Familia was intended to dominate everything in sight. In true Gothic competitive spirit it aimed at being bigger than anything else and certainly dwarfs Barcelona's own Gothic cathedral which was itself not completed until 1912.

Raised some twelve feet above the street, it was to be approached up flights of stairs and surrounded by a dry moat. The plan was a traditional Latin cross with a wide nave of five aisles and transepts of three aisles. The presbytery in the north was composed of seven chapels flanked by two sacristies and leading to a central chapel of the Assumption. In the south, on either side of the main entrance, were to be a baptistery and a confessional chapel.

There were two unconventional aspects of the plan, firstly, provision for a cloister to surround the whole church, serving both to insulate the church from street noise and to provide maximum processional space. Secondly, the sight of the main altar was not to be obstructed by the erection of a choir screen, but available to the whole of the congregation. This liturgical departure, which Gaudí had introduced into the restoration of Mallorca Cathedral (1904–14), was not without precedent; Santa Maria del Mar in Barcelona had the same arrangement dating from the late eighteenth century.

The main altar, raised six feet from the ground, was to be a simple table above which a crucifix surrounded with vine branches would be suspended. The nave, lit by large sixty-foot windows, would have been a forest of columns, each dedicated to a saint, apostle or bishop. These fluted stalk-like elements forked out at the top towards small hyperbolic domes, each with a central oculus to filter light through the branches. The church was to seat some 13,000 people on stone pews specially designed to inhibit the crossing of legs!

The three portals of the church were to have been the bible of the poor. The main entrance in the south, THE PORTAL OF THE GLORY, lit by the midday sun and designed to celebrate the resurrection, is the least documented part of the church. The nature of Gaudí's 1916–17 plans may in part be understood from Matamala's drawing. The iconography was to consist of scenes of the Kingdom of Heaven on the upper façade and scenes of man's attempt to reach such a heaven lower down. The main porch consisted of seven inclined columns with representations of the sins on their bases and of the virtues on the capitals. Behind each column was a door inscribed with part of the Lord's Prayer; the central column showed Adam and Eve and above them was a scene of Christ in the carpenter's shop to emphasize the Joseph cult.

(opposite)
The Sagrada Familia, Portal of the Nativity, front façade

The Sagrada Familia, Portal of the Glory, drawing by Matamala

The Sagrada Familia, Portal of the Passion, at the present (1976) stage of building

The terrace in front of this porch was to contain on the left, associated with the baptistery, a large fountain of four jets, representing the Rivers of Paradise, whilst on the right, a triple torchère symbolized the column of fire guiding the Children of Israel.

THE PORTAL OF THE PASSION for the west transept faces the setting sun. Designed by Gaudí around 1917, it was begun in 1960 under the supervision of Quintana and Puig Boada and has now reached the stage shown. The angular sloping struts with their tense ligaments express the agony of Christ's calvary and the harshness of sacrifice. The porch is divided into three, reading from left to right, the Portal of Faith, which is to contain scenes of Christ entering Jerusalem and being brought before Herod; the Portal of Charity with Jesus washing the disciples' feet, the last supper and the scene in the Garden of Gethsemane; and the Portal of Hope with Christ's humiliation, flagellation and crowning with thorns.

Only THE PORTAL OF THE NATIVITY in the east was constructed in Gaudí's lifetime, and its elaborate richness in part is explained by a generous donation made just before it was begun. It, too, is divided into three, from left to right, the Portals of Hope, Charity and Faith.

The Portal of Hope, devoted to the Virgin, shows scenes of the marriage of the Virgin and St. Joseph, the flight into Egypt and the massacre of the Innocents. It contains a palm-tree column supported by the web-footed tortoise from the Nile, a symbol of endurance, and is crowned by a motif taken from the rocks of Montserrat.

The central Portal of Charity, divided by a genealogical column tracing the descent from Abraham to Joseph, is dominated by the Bethlehem grotto studded with flowers, birds and stars and edged with melting snow. Above this rises the eternally green and incorruptible cypress tree, crowned with a 'Tau' cross, at its base a pelican symbolizing sacrifice.

The Portal of Faith on the right, devoted to St. Joseph, illustrates the stories of Christ in the Temple and Christ in the carpenter's shop. The palm column is supported this time by the claw-footed land tortoise from Palestine.

Pimpled, creased, ruffled, curled, pinched and fretted, the surface of the façade provides a constant irritation to the sense of touch. The figure groups themselves, in Ruskinian terms 'Fiction in solid substance', are relatable to the Catholic ideas of the sculptor Llimona and the

The Sagrada Familia, Portal of the Nativity, massacre of the Innocents from the Portal of Hope

The Sagrada Familia, Portal of the Nativity, web-footed sea tortoise of the Nile from the Portal of Hope

contemporary Artistic Circle of St. Luke. Until a recent revival of interest in nineteenth-century sculpture, these figures were very much out of favour with critical taste, and even George Collins called them 'dismal'. Gaudí's method of working is, however, of some interest. Like Pasolini after him, he auditioned his biblical epic from the people in the streets, a goatherd became Pontius Pilate, a rag and bone merchant, King Solomon. He photographed his chosen cast against a construction of mirrors which enabled him to record the effect from different view-points. Then, after experimenting with pose by the use of metals and wire skeletons, he made plaster casts of everybody and everything from flowers, fruit and grasses to chickens, snails and still-born children. Schweitzer recorded in his autobiography the trouble that was had in

(right)
The Sagrada Familia, the Rosary Portal. Gaudí's only comment on contemporary social unrest, this figure group portrays a potential anarchist being tempted with a bomb. The Portal was severely damaged during the Spanish Civil War.

The Sagrada Familia, Portal of the Nativity, cypress tree crowning the Portal of Charity

The Sagrada Familia, Portal of the Nativity, pelican at the base of the cypress tree from the Portal of Charity

finding a donkey for the flight into Egypt which was to result in the unfortunate animal being hoisted in the air to facilitate this awkward operation. From these casts plaster models were made, modified to the necessary scale, then put up on the façade in situ to study the effect. Further modifications would be made to allow for perspective distortion by the addition of material at various joints and, with the help of sculptural assistants, the final stone version cut and erected.

The dominant aspect of the whole concept from the start was the emphasis on verticality, the linking of heaven to earth. A central tower over the crossing was to rise some 557 feet and symbolize Christ; it was to be surrounded by four smaller towers, Matthew, Mark, Luke and John, the Evangelists. Each of the three façades was to have a further four bell towers, some 300 feet high, representing the twelve Disciples. On the Nativity façade these are Barnabas, Simon, Thaddeus and Mathias; begun about 1901, only Barnabas at the left was completed a few days before Gaudí's death. Streamlined ears of wheat or needle rocks from Montserrat contain helicoidal staircases symbolic of spiritual energy. This form, so characteristic of Gaudí, from the Mataró project to the chimneys of the Casa Milá, may well have been inspired by its appearance in Catalan Gothic architecture,

Photograph depicting Gaudí's use of mirrors in recording poses in sculpture on the Sagrada Familia

(opposite)
The Sagrada Familia, Portal of the Nativity, the Portal of Charity

Photograph of plaster casts for sculpture, including the donkey for the flight into Egypt from the Portal of the Nativity of the Sagrada Familia

(left and above)
The Sagrada Familia, interior views of the bell tower with the spiral staircase

The Sagrada Familia, detail of lipped openings on the bell tower

The Sagrada Familia, details of the finials from the apse

at its best in the choir at Morella, within easy reach of Tarragona. Each of these towers is a huge resonance chamber with lipped openings to deflect the sound to the ground. With the three sets of bell towers in operation a polyphony of normal bells and tubular bells operated electronically would have rung out over Barcelona, mixing with the sound of the wind and the 'happy sounds' of men in workshops grouped around the church. At their base sits the respective saint in a niche and crowning them are the famous baubled finials; spheres, truncated pyramids, octahedra, all interlocked and coated in Venetian glass mosaic. At one stage it was Gaudí's intention to surmount them with cherubim whose wings would be flexible and move with the wind. The towers are finally provided with inscriptions, reading vertically upwards, 'sursum corda [upwards the heart] sanctus, sanctus, sanctus, hosanna [in] excelsis'.

The picture of this enormous vision is completed by realizing that a large part of the church was to be coloured as is shown in the plaster model Gaudí exhibited in the 1910 Paris Exhibition. The Portal of Hope on the Nativity façade was to be green, symbolizing the Nile Valley, the centre Charity door was the brilliant blue of a Bethlehem night, the Portal of Faith, a burnt sienna representing the sands of Palestine. The triple 'sanctus' on the towers was in yellow, orange and red, the yellow light of the Father united with the martyred red of Christ through the mediation of the orange Holy Spirit. In the interior the right aisle of the nave was to be white and gold symbolic of joy and the left aisle painted with the purple and black of mourning.

Gaudí provided plans for artificial illumination almost as if he had seen the shafts of light around Feininger's visionary woodcut *The Cathedral of Socialism* for the 1919 Bauhaus manifesto. Double electric beams were to be hidden in the polyhedron sections half-way up the finials where the holes can still be seen, one beam directed towards the centre tower, the other shining towards the ground, a metaphor for the Gospel falling on mankind.

Uncharitable reminders that very little of this has been achieved may perhaps be silenced by Ruskin's words, 'It is not the church we want, but the sacrifice, not the gift but the giving'. The 'ruins' are to be valued as a residue of faith and adoration.

A Critical Assessment

Throughout the nineteenth century the collapse of cohesive systems of belief, changing patterns of education, increasing social and geographic mobility and the establishment of new systems of patronage, all made for a situation in which the architect, along with the painter and sculptor, was faced with new assumptions, new priorities of taste and, most importantly, with new personal responsibility of choice in matters of style.

At the same time as the authority of unifying cultural patterns was being eroded, an increased awareness of history was apparent with progress being made throughout the century in matters of prestige and methodology. This abundant knowledge of models from the past was made more accessible to visual artists by the parallel advancements in reproductive techniques. By the end of the century the architect had the opportunity as never before of solving doubts and problems by referring to his 'museum without walls'. He could sit in his office with his books and magazines and employ a 'pick and mix' philosophy of design. This facility was obviously available to Gaudí, and he made use of it, borrowing from many different periods at many different levels from surface details to matters of principal or structural solutions. More important, however, than identifying such quotations is the realization that essentially Gaudí was a hand and eye worker; influences coming to him second hand through the printed page were absorbed by the resources of direct experience. His eclecticism was kept vital by the depth of his looking at the world about him and by his direct and intimate handling of materials.

To understand Gaudí's architecture is to understand the unmeasurable elements, the nature of Roman Catholicism, the Catalan temperament, the qualities of the Catalan landscape, aspects which need to be experienced and are largely resistant to explanation.

'The man without religion is a man spiritually ruined, a mutilated man', Gaudí is reported to have declared. Here was the credit of faith which gave his work substance, confidence, credibility. There is little tolerance of doubt in Gaudí's world.

National characteristics are difficult to assess, yet if he is compared with fellow Spanish artists in the field of painting, Picasso, Miró and Dali, similar qualities are revealed.* He shares with them a shameless fertility, a healthy sensuousness, a sense of fun and a wilful unorthodoxy. In particular, like Picasso he had a keen eye and a warm physical grasp, like Miró his personal sense of fantasy was illuminated by nature and rooted in the soil, and like Dali he was obsessed with the 'realization' of his visions.

Catalonia, especially the country around Tarragona, is very fertile, and there is no doubt that Gaudí drew constantly on his love and knowledge of this particular landscape for inspiration. His borrowings were often very direct, from the palm frond of the Vicens iron railing to the cypress tree of the Nativity façade, from the pine-cone shapes of the small turrets at the side of the Nativity façade to the palm-tree bark influencing the texture of columns at Santa Coloma. A visit to the sandstone needle rocks of Montserrat, near Barcelona, or to the meandering vine terraces stepping the land with dry stone walls around Tarragona, confirms this local relevance. Responses from nature are a basic ingredient in Gaudí's art.

With priorities established, theoretical influences can now be discussed. Gaudí had little time for abstract thinking and was not himself a theorist. His early statement on 'Ornamentation', preserved in the municipal library at Reus, must not be over-estimated. It was written in 1878 before he had built anything and when he had not yet fully assimilated the ideas of his teachers. Equally, any urge to collect his subsequent dogmatic aphorisms, reported in the main at second hand, into a consistent theory is to be resisted. His familiarity with books, one imagines, was neither more nor less than that of any educated professional man.

Even admitting that Gaudí was no intellectual, it is interesting to consider the relationship to two thinkers, the English art critic John Ruskin (1819–1900) and the French Neo-Gothic architect and theorist Eugène-Emanuel Viollet-le-Duc (1814–79). A discussion of their ideas will be valuable in returning Gaudí to the context of nine-

*Miró and Dali are both Catalans; Picasso, born in Malaga, moved to Barcelona at the age of fourteen and spent a large part of his formative years there.

teenth-century thinking from which he has too often been ripped. Reading is as much a confirmatory as well as an inspirational activity and to talk of 'influence', with regard to Ruskin, may be dangerous. If Gaudí did read his books it is likely that the approach was an emotional one, he would have read what he wanted to read and taken what suited his purpose.

Gaudí and Ruskin

Ruskin was certainly known in Barcelona at the turn of the century. Fontanals, a leading figure in the revival of Catalan literature, whose lectures we know Gaudí attended, had been in contact with the Pre-Raphaelites and could have promoted an interest in English aesthetics. Güell himself, an Anglophile, would very likely have returned from business trips to England with news and literature. In 1901, L'Avenç provided the first translation into Catalan of selections of the English critic's writings in a cheap popular edition, and this was followed by a more extensive anthology in 1903. Both were translated by Cebriá Montoliu, who was chiefly concerned with Ruskin's natural history and geological interests, dividing his larger books into such sections dealing with sky, mountains, stones, water, flowers. Apart from this emphasis, Ruskin was also introduced to a Spanish audience as a political economist. Sesame and the Lilies was translated into Catalan in 1905 and into Spanish in 1907, and Unto This Last and Munera Pulvis were also available by this time. Unfortunately, it must be admitted that Ruskin's most important writings on architecture, The Seven Lamps (1849) and The Stones of Venice (1851–53), were not available until later, and even then Gaudí would have had to rely on French translations.*

Had Ruskin ever been witness to Gaudí's work doubtless the full force of his invective would have been unleashed. At the very least he would have accused him of impurity. The use of direct casting from life would have gained his disapproval as a mechanical activity, and the inscriptions on many of the buildings would have been censured as illegible. This said, Gaudí's architecture is profoundly Ruskinian.

Gaudí can be seen as answering Ruskin's call made in the preface to The Seven Lamps for 'the good man to fight the blasphemies of the contemporary earth', one who realized as Ruskin did that 'good' architecture could only come about through commitment, belief and altruism. Gaudí can be recognized as the prime example

*The Seven Lamps was translated into French by George Elwall in 1901, but there is no evidence that Gaudí would have had access to this. Apart from the extract, 'The Lamp of Obedience', translated into Catalan as part of an anthology by Cebriá Montoliu in 1901, it must be admitted that Gaudí may perhaps not have had access to this text until the French edition of 1916. As far as I know The Seven Lamps was never translated into Spanish. The Stones of Venice was translated into French firstly in 1906 by Mathilde P. Cremieux, but it was probably not until the 1912 French translation that it was easily available. A Spanish version, without, unfortunately, the important section entitled 'The Nature of Gothic', was published in Madrid but with no publishing date.

of an architect with a sense of mission and his Sagrada Familia as an enormous symbol of goodness and self-sacrifice, a definite plus on the credit side of man's spirituality.

Gaudí combined the Ruskinian image of the architect as master-builder working in the mason's yard along with his men, humbly capable of turning his hand to all aspects of building, with the equally Ruskinian goal of raising building to the status of architecture by being both painter and sculptor. He built from feeling, scorning measurement and calculation and whenever possible relying on sensitive adjustment, just as Ruskin advocated in The Stones of Venice, 'exactly so far as architecture works on known rules and from given models, it is not an art but a manufacture'.

Gaudí would have agreed with Ruskin's judgement that the value of any art work, painting, sculpture or architecture, resides in the degree to which it is an image, indeed a celebration, of natural creation, in proportion to its 'fullness of life'. In order to equip him to achieve this, the architect, according to Ruskin, must be sent to the hills for 'affectionate observation' of the forms of geology. He must study the flower as a model of proportion and examine the rigid strength of tree branches.

Not only was architecture to refer to nature, but it was to partake of the same 'organic vitality' as nature by being itself analogous to an organism. We are to consider our building, says Ruskin, 'as a kind of organized creature'. To this end the architect must study the structure of animal bones; 'there is', he writes in 'The Lamp of Truth', 'a certain organisation in the management of such parts [of a building] like that of the continuous bones of a skeleton', yet just as the outer surface of the human frame conceals much of its anatomy, we must not mind if the architect conceals his framework, as Gaudí did most obviously in the Casa Milá. The surface is equally important, like the scales of an animal's skin; remove it, and the building is dead. These emotional metaphors would have been totally in sympathy with Gaudí's thinking.

Despite borrowings, Gaudí's architecture was far from being Gothic, yet it contained all the personality characteristics which Ruskin ascribes to that style in The Stones of Venice, savageness, changefulness, grotesqueness, rigidity, naturalism and redundancy. It is interesting to consider Gaudí's buildings in the light of these values which Ruskin defines in the following way.

SAVAGENESS:
'A rudeness', 'a waywardness', 'anti-authoritarian', 'constantly fighting orthodoxy and etiquette', 'full of wolfish life'.

CHANGEFULNESS:
'A flexibility to needs', a pragmatic opportunism, a style which can 'shrink into a turret, expand into a hall, coil into a staircase, or spring into a spire. Subtle and flexible like a fiery serpent.'

GROTESQUENESS:
A tendency to delight in 'fantastic ludicrous images'.

RIGIDITY:
'A stiffness analogous to that of the bones of a limb or the fibres of a tree.'

NATURALISM:
'A love of veracity': the introduction in decoration of the most familiar and commonplace incidents of daily life. The architect must not be obscure, he must talk about the vegetation and the world which people see every day.

REDUNDANCY:
'The uncalculated bestowal of wealth and labour', the result of sacrifice, 'a magnificent enthusiasm which feels it never could do enough to reach the fullness of its ideal.' 'A profound sympathy with the fullness and wealth of the material universe.' This quality certainly seems relevant in assessing the Sagrada Familia sculpture, and, in the minds of both Ruskin and Gaudí, such a clutter was an index of humility and made the work more acceptable to common appeal. No architecture, warns Ruskin, is so haughty as that which is simple; the Sagrada Familia was intended as a church for the people.

Apart from sharing ethical and sentimental assumptions, Gaudí could have found in Ruskin confirmation of actual practice. In particular there would have been encouragement to employ human craft skills in fighting the evil of mindless industrialization, justification for the use of colour in promoting 'the reality' of architecture and endorsement of the value of shadow in providing a building with a sense of power, a truth which Gaudí demonstrated so clearly in the knitted brows of the Casa Milá. Finally there would have been support for the important role architecture was playing in the movement for Catalan nationalism. Architecture, says Ruskin, 'is expressive of race', 'it can give identity, and promote obedience, unity, fellowship and order.' 'Noble architecture is an embodiment of the polity, life, history and religious faith of nations.'

Ruskin provides appropriate criteria for judging Gaudí's work. The questions to ask are, 'Was it done with enjoyment?' 'Has it through richness of record become a memorial?' 'Is it affecting?' 'There is a crust', he writes in 'The Lamp of Power', 'about the impressible parts of men's minds, which must be pierced through, before they can be touched to the quick; and though we may pick at it and scratch it in a thousand separate places, we might as well have let it alone if we do not come through somewhere with a deep thrust.' Nobody can doubt the reality of Gaudí's thrust, he was not an architect ever to stop short, his whole career was an example of that prolonged giving of one's utmost which Ruskin demanded.

Gaudí and Viollet-le-Duc

Gaudí had been in direct contact with Prof. Rogent, head of the Barcelona School of Architecture and with the architects, Villar and Martorell, all of whom were admirers of Viollet-le-Duc. It was no doubt their encouragement which caused Viollet's books in the school library to be exceptionally well thumbed. On one of his rare trips outside Catalonia, Gaudí went to Carcassonne at the time when Viollet was beginning the restorations of that city and was so absorbed in studying the work, so the story goes, that locals mistook him for the French master.

Viollet was an agnostic, an advocate of reason and a champion of modern materials. Gaudí was a believer, a man of feeling and, with the exception of tentative use of reinforced concrete, a traditionalist in materials. The massive ten volumes of Viollet's *Dictionnaire raisonné*, while specifically related to French architecture, are an A to Z of practical information, and it is known that Gaudí borrowed a volume from his friend Cabañas and returned it with annotations in the margin.

The two volumes of the *Entretiens*, published in 1863 and 1872, were more discursive and, while not as sympathetic as Ruskin's writing, would have provided Gaudí with interesting ideas. It is usual to emphasize the influence of Viollet in terms of his structural analysis of Gothic architecture, yet what is equally dominant in these books is his admiration for Greek art. Reading the *Entretiens* could well have created a Greek-Gothic hybrid as an intellectual pin-up and account for Gaudí's subsequent paradoxical description of the Sagrada Familia as a 'Hellenistic temple of Mediterranean Gothic'.

According to Viollet, the Gothic was a 'democratic style', a style of the laity. The architect, sculptor and painter were 'Les enfants du peuple' and the building the result of 'enfranchized labour'. The Gothic of the early thirteenth century was 'An awakening of the ancient Gallic [i.e. national] spirit', arising out of and expressive of 'a desire for political consolidation', as it pioneered a route towards light and liberty. True or not, this was fighting talk for Gaudí and Catalan nationalism.

The Gothic was seen as a style of interconnections, a kind of architectural ecology. Like Ruskin, Viollet stresses the idea of organism, declaring that in Gothic 'there is not a form or a process that is not produced by the necessity of the organism'. It was the continuation of this kind of argument which made Gaudí criticize the use of buttresses as crutches. They could only be seen as evidence for the essential imperfection and weakness of the organism.

Without being a religious man, Viollet accepts that to build a cathedral was 'the supreme task of the architect' and that the artists of the Middle Ages had tackled one of the most difficult problems, 'How can men be led to conceive of a building as the dwelling place of the Christian God?' He provides his readers with the answer: 'They made their church an epitome, as it were, of the creation, an assemblage of all created things . . . a sort of universal epic in stone. If the undertaking was difficult, who shall censure those who attempted it?' What clearer challenge, programme and final apology could be found for the Sagrada Familia?

'Between the Gothic master mason and the Greek builder was a mode of feeling and expression in common,' Viollet tells his readers in Lecture VII of the *Entretiens*. Both shared an interest in light, albeit developed differently; both were involved in a 'complete expression', 'a total concept of the arts'.

The particular characteristic of the Greeks was their power of 'realization', their ability to make myths real. They were also especially brilliant at the 'mise-en-scène'. 'The Greek architect,' says Viollet, 'does not level the rock on which his edifice is to be built, he embellishes it and takes advantage of its asperities.' In other words, the Greeks worked with nature in a spirit of collaboration. In just such a spirit did the 'Montana Pelada' become Gaudí's acropolis, one example from many of his care and sensitivity to siting.

Viollet also highlights more practical aspects of Greek genius: their awareness that buildings are not always viewed straight on and that therefore they must be made agreeable from all aspects; their awareness too that perspective and the problems of perception can result in the diminishing of a building's impact. Such visual erosion can be counteracted by special attention being given to corner angles, by the modifying of proportions and by the use of colour, which, at the hands of the Greeks, according to Viollet, was 'strong and vivid'.

From Viollet Gaudí could have been encouraged to think about a total unified approach, not only in the mutual interdependence of structural units but also in the use of decoration. 'One of the charms of good architecture,' writes Viollet, 'consists in a close relationship between the external and the internal ornamentation.' 'The external ornamentation should prepare the spectator for and prefigure to him, that which he will find within.' This theme and variations approach has already been discussed in the Casa Milá and the Palau Güell, which Gaudí himself is said to have described as 'meagre Viollet-le-Duc'.

In addition to accepting some generalized aims from Viollet, Gaudí would also have mentally underlined certain practical observations. He would have found verbal support for the contemporary use of brick, perhaps first seen in Barcelona in Fontseré's conservatory for the Ciudadela Park (1872). 'Why employ stone,' writes Viollet, 'when we might with greater economy make use of a material which offers so many advantages, facility in transport and lifting, lightness, perfect adhesion to plastering, dryness and unlimited durability.'

If the fashionable example of Arabic art was not enough inducement there was also approval of ceramic tiles. 'Why,' he asks, 'in our palaces and mansions should we forgo the use of glazed terracotta . . . . By the judicious use of faience we could effect a saving in stone sufficient to compensate for the extra cost of these coatings.'

In Lecture XVII, Viollet reminds modern architects of the need for adequate ventilation; they must, he says, be aware of those necessary 'few cubic yards of fresh air' and simply opening windows is not good enough, such primitive methods result in colds or inflammation of the lungs [!]. Architects ought to bend their minds to this problem; Gaudí seems to have taken up the challenge, mindful not only of providing for example adequate ventilation of the basement stables at the Palau Güell, but also ingeniously providing holes underneath the windows of the Casa Batlló, a primitive form of air-conditioning.

The most interesting hint Gaudí might have picked up from his reading of Viollet is the discussion of tilted structures in Lecture XII. Here Viollet clearly states, 'The use of rigid shafts or cast-iron columns as oblique supports is a means of which our builders have not yet thought, I hardly know why . . . . substituting oblique for vertical resistance is a principle which . . . may assume a very high degree of importance.' He adds that while this contravenes orthodoxy, yet a new architecture may be found by relying on such 'novel principles of structure'. It would have been typical of Gaudí's thinking to have transferred Viollet's metal supports into brick and stone.

Illustration from Viollet-le-Duc's Entretiens *depicting oblique iron columns used in the design for a market place*

Working Method

Gaudí's success was in no small way due to the excellence of his working relationships. Like an orchestral conductor, he achieved the difficult balance between dominance and collaboration, drawing the best out of his assistants and allowing their individual talents to develop without losing sight of his own overall vision.

Ironically, his working method came closer to the soft-focus vision of the medieval 'bauhütten', called for by Gropius, than anything which was achieved at the Weimar Bauhaus. 'There is no essential difference between the artist and the craftsman. . . . Let us create a new guild of craftsmen,' states the 1919 Bauhaus manifesto. Gaudí, certainly in his work for the Sagrada Familia, had done just this, creating around him a group of trusted craftsmen who looked to him as master mason and director of operations. This group was held together by belief in Gaudí, respect for each other's skills and the soundly exercised reflexes of craft traditions.

Despite a slightly shifting constitution of assistants, for most of his mature career Gaudí knew loyal and trusted helpers, men like Berenguer and Jujol, architects in their own right, the sculptors Matamala and Carlos Mani, the plaster specialist Bertran and the ironsmith Lluís Badia. It would be easy to overdo the medieval dream, but certainly Gaudí seems to have come closer to it than any other architect in the modern world.

Gaudí was not an abstract thinker; he limited theory to a minimum. Vision was there, pre-established, recorded sometimes in fluid impressionistic sketches, but the realization came about only with direct involvement with materials. The strengths of his method lay in constant vigilance during construction, empirical testing of materials, sound intuition based on experience and a flexibility made possible through a shared faith between architect and assistant, allowing for spontaneous on-site decisions and adaptions.

Gaudí obviously was as capable as any professionally trained architect to design with paper, pen and mathematics, relying on measurement and calculation. Sometimes bureaucracy would not be cowed by Gaudí's personal brand of fearless autocracy and demanded accurate pre-planning. However, where faith in his abilities permitted freedom, Gaudí took it, freedom to move away from the drawing board, freedom to change and modify in the course of execution.

Gaudí was a model maker, partly because it accorded, one imagines, with his three-dimensional grasp of a building from the very start and partly in sympathy with the many now anonymous workers who must have been necessary to realize his ideas, men who could be relied upon to interpret an actual visualization much better than a two-dimensional plan. Most of these models in wood and plaster of whole buildings or details, such as chimneys or staircases, have been lost or destroyed. A visit to the Sagrada Familia workshops today can still evoke this method of working.

Structure

Recently criticism has tended to emphasize structural concerns in Gaudí's work. Perucho, for example, says categorically, that 'the ornamental or symbolic effect of Gaudí's architecture was not its principal impulse, which must go to structure.' Such niceties of drawing room precedence misunderstand the situation. As the organic analogies make clear, both aspects are equally important. A skin without a suitable bone-structure is a cripple, and a flayed corpse is not only unattractive but remarkably inefficient. There are, however, three interrelated aspects of structure which it is useful to isolate: the parabola, the tilted column and the tile vault.

The *parabolic arch* made an early appearance in Gaudí's work and was used most confidently as a decorative form in the entrances of the Palau Güell, although its structural use had already been suggested in the Mataró workshop, the garden fountain of the Casa Vicens and the stable block for the Güell Pavilions. It was to reach its full development on the top floor of the Casa Milá, in the Passion façade of the Sagrada Familia and in the model for the church at Santa Coloma. Despite being a basic characteristic of Gaudí's style, it does not seem possible to pin-point its derivation; certainly it was not part of contemporary architectural usage.

The parabolic or catenary curve is not a geometrical curve. It is the path obtained when a string suspended from its two ends finds equilibrium, seen more clearly perhaps in the trajectory of a jet of water. In both examples, the forces of gravity are acting evenly along the resulting curves. Incorporated into an architectural system, it contravenes accepted premises of the traditional post and beam or column and arch systems. Firstly, there is no transition from one direction to another as in the former, nor springing or climaxing as in the latter. Its use would therefore imply a smoothly continuous style without critical tensions. Secondly, as the arms of the parabola splay outwards, it does not meet a ground plane at a 90° angle.

It was a rule of respectable architecture that all load-forces should be verticalized by the time they reached the ground. The *tilted column* suggested a measure of impermanence and insecurity. Tilting, leaning and propping, while satisfactory for the plebeian 'lean-to' or the tent, were not within the etiquette of fine architecture.

Where necessary, as in Gothic architecture, lateral thrusts were contained by the use of buttresses. Gaudí saw such methods as an artificiality. He de-corsetted the Gothic and accepted the sag as natural. Inevitably at the time this was regarded as sloppy, ugly and unbecoming a professional. Gaudí gathered justification for such reasoning by studying the growth of trees, the lean of trunks and the inclination of branches as they proportionally support and distribute forces and weights. The tilted columns of the Park Güell and the crypt of Santa Coloma were, therefore, adopted from direct observation of natural laws and from a critical assessment of the weaknesses of the Gothic style. They were already suggested in his use of the parabola, and they might even have been slightly cued by an exaggerated use of what the Greeks called 'entasis', giving a subtly calculated inclination to a column in order to correct perspective distortion. At the very beginning of his career Gaudí had indeed planned that the porch columns for 'El Capricho' should be inclined, and his treatment of the Doric colonnade at the Park Güell clearly suggests this source.

The third element is the *tile vault*, seen most clearly in the Sagrada Familia Schools (see p. 65) and the top floor roof of the Casa Milá. The exact derivation of this method is unknown, although it can be found in the vaults of Mesopotamia and Egypt. Despite claiming such successes as the famous Sistine Chapel, the system was little used in the modern world outside Catalonia and had come to be accepted as a vernacular technique.

Basically, the system consists of a series of laminations made from broad terracotta tiles, laid flat and stuck together with an especially strong mortar. The vault or roof so constructed is therefore not held together by the pressure of gravity but by cohesion. It relies on very skilled workmen but has several advantages; it is light, non-combustible, has good load-bearing properties, is very flexible and can be used to create very complex shapes. It can also be erected without expensive wooden scaffolding by being so strong that the builders working overhand can support themselves on the previous day's masonry. Gaudí was not the only contemporary architect to up-grade this vernacular technique, and the main champion of this cohesive system of architecture was Guastavino, who as early as the 1880s exported its use to America, where it enjoyed considerable success until skilled labour costs made it uneconomical.

In using the tile vault, strength of shape is far more important than intrinsic strength of the materials used, and from this fact Gaudí, using this traditional technique, developed the surfaces of double curvature which have recently seemed so relevant for contemporary architectural developments.

Such surfaces as the hyperbolic paraboloid (one line moving over two others) seen on the Casa Milá roof and in the projected nave vaults of the Sagrada Familia can be reduced to mathematical equations, and the fact that they are generated by straight lines makes construction simpler and cheaper. Equally important, however, for Gaudí's way of thinking, is the fact that they could also be seen in nature, for example, in the undulations of the 'Tridacna' shell and in the hollow of the human back as it twists at the waist. He is even supposed to have found religious significance in this form explaining the generation of the hyperbolic paraboloid as representing the Father and Son being united by means of the Holy Spirit.

Architecture as Synthesis

Having isolated three ingredients of Gaudí's style out of context, it is necessary to emphasize that his architecture is the result of a complex synthesis acting on more than one level.

Firstly, he accepted the trinity of painting, sculpture and architecture. He combined invention in both two and three dimensions with the functions of practical habitation and at his best rose above the limitations of the separate arts to become a total creator. In the preface to *The Stones of Venice* Ruskin declares, with his usual authoritative conviction, that 'The architect who [is] not a sculptor or a painter [is] nothing better than a frame-maker on a large scale,' and this was a goal which was still being called for in the 1919 Bauhaus manifesto. 'Let us conceive . . . the new building of the future which will embrace architecture, painting, and sculpture in one unity.'

Secondly, Gaudí adhered to the belief that the architect's responsibility extended beyond the creation of spaces to a full concern for everything which went into those spaces. He believed that the architect's sphere of operation should include furniture, light-fittings and door-handles in the interest of producing a total internal and external unity. This kind of attitude, demanding the combination of various skills, was shared by many architects in the late nineteenth century, including Mackintosh, van de Velde and Guimard. It was partly a response to the evils of fragmentation and division of labour brought about by industrialization and partly a natural result of an 'organic' approach demanding a total system of interconnections, in which the smallest element echoed the whole.

Finally, on a more ambiguous level, Gaudí's architecture provides a synthesis of sensory attractions, a correspondence of emotions, ideas and sensations and the enrichment of one sense by the vicarious triggering of another. Gaudí's architecture is intensely visual yet it seduces more than the eyes. Dali has referred to its ability to water the taste buds referring to its 'comestible' nature. The variety and richness of touch experiences is one of its constant joys, and the value of musical rhythm was so important to Gaudí that even as late as 1916 he attended professional classes on Gregorian chant.

This conscious dialogue between the senses was of course a feature of late nineteenth-century thinking. Barcelona was very sympathetic to Wagner's music, and his concept of the 'gesamtkunstwerk', the total art work, could hardly fail to have been discussed in its intellectual and artistic circles. A more surprising source for such thinking is Viollet-le-Duc. In the first lecture of the *Entretiens*, 'synaesthesia' is discussed clearly and without mystique. 'Architecture and music are twins,' Viollet declares, 'the architect must be alive to melody' and by producing a composite of sights, sounds and ideas he will enrich awareness and arrive at 'the complete expression.'

The Mongrel Crust

A style of such rich responses, which involves so many details combined into a credible whole, inevitably implies great sophistication. In contrast, however, there is a group of qualities in Gaudí's work which may be called his mongrel crust, qualities of vulgarity, crudeness and ingenuousness.

Whether it be in his reliance on vernacular brick-laying skills, or in the influence of the popular Christmas manger scenes called 'Pessebres' on the Sagrada Familia sculpture, Gaudí never forgot his local dialect. The slanting columns suggesting the improvised prop and his use of cheap materials, descending the scale of values to include broken bottles, rubble and whitewash, all amount to a quick injection of slang to invigorate a tired and self-satisfied architectural etiquette.

Gaudí's buildings are not 'haute couture', they could not be called well-tailored; at times he embraced what amounts to a knowing primitivism, seen in the pseudo 'lair' of the Casa Milá or the rough cut cave-shelter of the Santa Coloma crypt. This attitude, shared by certain painters and sculptors of the time in Europe, was a self-conscious corrective to a surfeit of refinement and culture, a romantic upholding of the values of raw innocence. Gaudí himself once declared 'Originality means to return to the origin.' Gaudí always retained some childlike aspects. Despite mature disillusionment, he preserved his optimism and his joyful sense of wonder. There was a side to his nature which liked the glittering, the brash, the boisterous, and certainly in some of his 'playground' spaces, such as the Casa Milá roof, bug-eyed monsters from fun-land are only just around the corner. Here is popular entertainment and popular appeal, a truly 'vulgar' style made possible only through the generosity of a financial élite.

Images and Paradoxes

Gaudí's buildings provide the history of architecture with some of its strongest images. Within these images are combined pride and humility, collaboration and dominance, sophistication and vulgarity, humour and grandeur. Despite the generosity of detail, each building never loses an overall peculiarity, each one has individuality, impact and is hugely memorable. This quality of image-strength enables his works to give identity to place and promotes affection. Irrespective of its artistic achievement, Gaudí's Sagrada Familia *is* Barcelona as much, for example, as Gilbert's Eros fountain *is* Piccadilly Circus.

Like many other ascetics, Gaudí was also a sensualist. His architecture is for grasping eyes; eyes which feel and hold, which bite into surfaces and slide around fluid corners, which thrill as they bump over incrustations and delight themselves in maze-like complexity. To experience Gaudí's work is to put the eyes in a gymnasium where they jump, run, move through, make connections and are kept constantly active.

In his comments on Gothic Flamboyant architecture,

Ruskin writes, 'When construction became principal . . . and story subordinate, the shaft and the arch rib became everything and the wall nothing', resulting in 'a mere osseus thorax of a building instead of a living body.' Nobody knew the truth of this more than Gaudí. He never forgot the flesh and skin of his buildings, nor the sense of 'story' they could express. His robust manipulation of wall surfaces is doubtless to be set against a vernacular tradition of pushing and pulling façades by indenting them with recessed windows and doorways and letting balconies project from them. In such common usage, however, the plane of the wall remains flat and static, unlike Gaudí's, where the plane is interrupted and the wall allowed to live with enormous sculptural force.

Gaudí's repertory of forms was especially wide; the sheer generosity of his inventiveness, his refusal to re-employ formula solutions is remarkable even when set within the immediate context of Barcelona, which probably contains more head-turning architectural astonishment than any other European city. A consideration of his treatment of corners or a catalogue of his various columns would evidence this fertility.

Gaudí's mastery of flow and interruption and his control of the dynamics of spiralling, cornering and stepping may perhaps only be understood in time. What is immediately obvious is the richness and variety of his surfaces. He constantly modified the skin of his buildings, not only in terms of colour and texture, but also in terms of light sensitivity, playing a full gamut from surfaces which seem light-porous and soak up the sunshine to those which bounce it blindingly back from jewel-like facets. The hard, spikey cruelty of iron contrasts with the soft polishable sensuousness of wood, the slow crumbling informality of soft rubble is set against the clean, swift brightness of glazed ceramic.

Casanelles has nicely tagged Gaudí as a 'realistic dreamer'. In this paradox lies the heart of his achievement and the explanation of his appeal to Surrealism. Unlike the architects of German Expressionism, Finsterlin, Scheerbart and Taut, Gaudí's visions did not remain on the drawing board. Their work was in the main abortive, his saw the light of day and his dreams were realized. Equally Gaudí is to be distinguished from other 'realistic dreamers,' men like Cheval, Simon Rodia, Clarence Schmidt. Like them, he allowed architecture to satisfy personal obsessions, sharing with them a function of intimacy and a psychological dimension. However, whereas they were amateurs whose achievement must ultimately be explained in terms of self-referential therapy, Gaudí was a professional balancing his own personal needs with a strong sense of service.

What impresses about Gaudí is that while his architecture provides such an effective sounding board for subjective emotions, it is equally full of practical commonsense, the kind of commonsense which made him consult the prevailing wind patterns when designing the early Mataró Cooperative project, to ensure that houses suffered the least amount of pollution from the factory chimneys, or the commonsense which in the Casa Batlló results in his setting some of the doors within larger hinged doors, normally closed, but which can be opened on special occasions, for example, to facilitate furniture removals (see p. 57).

Any assessment of Gaudí's achievement must take into account three factors. Firstly, he was fortunate in meeting Güell early in his career, not only for the faith the patron had in his abilities and which allowed for freedom, but also for the subsequent introduction to other textile patrons. Secondly, an 'appui moral' existed in the social and political situation so that he was building at a time and in a place where personal prestige could be amplified by national prestige. Thirdly, there was the richness of Catalan craft traditions which Gaudí could and did rely upon. These awarenesses in no way detract from Gaudí's own success. They are a further measure of his pragmatism, his ability to estimate what was possible and to make the most of local opportunities. They therefore become the roots of his specialness.

Gaudí is one of the few architects whose discovery can promote enjoyment as well as respect. In his work there is courage, generosity and joy, values directly communicable through instinct and intuition, immensely affirmative of his humanity. Gaudí's buildings must not be copied by contemporary enthusiasts either in terms of forms or techniques, but they should be experienced as examples of other possibilities born of alternative priorities.

Chronology

Gaudí

1852	June 25: Antoni Gaudí i Cornet was born at Reus (?) in the province of Tarragona.
1863	After preliminary schooling under the elder Berenguer, proceeded with his secondary education in Reus.
1867–69	Project with friends Toda and Ribera for restoration of Cistercian monastery at Poblet.
1869	Received his Bachillerato.
1869–72	June: began pre-university studies at Convent of Carmelites (converted into School of Sciences), Barcelona.
1873	September: admitted to the School of Architecture, Barcelona University. Began to obtain part-time work from the architects, Villar, Sala, and Martorell, from the master-builder Fontseré, and from the industrial machinery firm, Padrós y Borrás.
1875	Project design for water tank to service Citadel Park.
1876	Gaudí's mother, Antonia, died. Collaboration with Villar for the Lady Chapel of monastery at Montserrat (cf. illus. Rafols, 1929, p. 13).
1876–79	Gaudí's diary (now kept at Reus Museum).
1876–82(?)	Collaboration with Josep Fontseré on work for Citadel Park.
1877–78	Final degree examinations; 15 March 1878: received his degree in Madrid.
1878	Study on 'Ornamentation' (Reus Museum); opened his architectural office, Calle del Call 11.3°; designed and constructed a desk for himself; pew and other furniture for Pantheon Chapel of marqués de Comillas at Santander; working for Martorell; Paris World Fair: exhibited a showcase for the glove manufacturer, Comella, and the housing project for Mataró.
1878–79	Won municipal competition for street lamps, now in Plaza Real.
1878–85(?)	Working with friend, Emilio Cabañas, for textile cooperative at Mataró.
1879	Gaudí joined Catalan Association of Scientific Excursions.
1879–83	Several commissions from local religious associations, including altar decorations, lighting and furniture for Jesus Maria College, San Paciano parish, part of floor mosaic remains.
1882	Project for hunting lodge at Garraf commissioned by Güell.
1883	Visit to Banyuls, Elna, Carcassonne; recommended by Martorell to succeed Villar as architect of the Sagrada Familia church; began work on the crypt.
1883–85	House for Vicens, Barcelona: remodelled 1924-27 by Serra Martinez; fountain in

garden destroyed c. 1947 (cf. Collins, 1960, illus. 10); recently restored by Antonio Pineda; house for Máximo Diaz de Quijano, Comillas in province of Santander: construction supervised by Cristobal Cascante.

1884–88   Güell Pavilions: gate, stables, porter's lodge; work on the estate included a decorative brick staircase, now destroyed.

1885   Altar for Bocabella, the instigator of the Sagrada Familia; 19 March: first mass celebrated in crypt of Sagrada Familia, St. Joseph's Day.

1885–90   Güell Palace, now a theatre museum.

1887   Trip to Andalusia and Morocco with the second marqués de Comillas; crypt of the Sagrada Familia was vaulted.

1887–93   Commissioned by Bishop Grau to build new episcopal palace in Astorga; work stopped in 1893 on death of the bishop; later roofed by Luís de Guereta.

1888   Moorish Pavilion of Compañia Transatlantica exhibited at Barcelona International Exhibition: modification of similar pavilion exhibited the previous year at Cadiz Naval Exhibition where it was attributed to G. Cabezas.

1889–94   Convent and School of Santa Teresa, Barcelona; an additional later project for a chapel (1908–10) was never executed.

1891–94   House of 'Los Botines' for Fernandez y Andrés, León; lower floor now occupied by a bank.

1892   Completion of apse wall for Sagrada Familia; work begun on the Nativity façade.

1892–93   Project for Spanish Franciscan mission in Tangiers.

1898   Commission received for church at Santa Coloma de Cervelló.

1898–1900 +   Calvet House; awarded Town Council prize, 1900.

1900–01   Towers of the Nativity façade, Sagrada Familia begun.

1900–02   Enclosing wall and gate for the estate of Hermenegildo Miralles, built by Sugrañes; the roof of the gateway has been removed and the iron railing was removed in 1959 (cf. Collins, 1960, illus. 73); 'Bellesguard', Barcelona, for Maria Segués.

1900–14   Park Güell on 'Montana Pelada'; now a public park with the house built by Berenguer now housing the Gaudí Museum.

1902   Interior decorations for Café Torino, Barcelona (cf. Martinell, 1975, illus. 353).

1904   Project of house for painter, Luís Graner (cf. Martinell, 1975, illus. 354–5), which anticipated rounded room spaces; storage shed for José Badia, Calle de Napoles, Barcelona (cf. Martinell, 1975, illus. 363), now destroyed.

1904–05   First Glorious Mystery for monumental rosary at Montserrat; collaboration with sculptor José Llimona; Gaudí's project has now been modified.

1904–06   Remodelled Batlló House, Barcelona.

1904–14   Restorations and modifications of cathedral, Palma de Mallorca, together with J. Rubió and J. M. Jujol (cf. Emilio Sagrista, *Gaudí en la Catedral de Mallorca*, 1962).

1905   Pulpits for parochial church, Blanes, near Gerona.

1906   Gaudí's father, Francisco, died.

1906–10   Milá House, Barcelona: collaboration with Canaleta, Sugrañes and Jujol; 1954: F. Juan Barba Corsini converted attic floor into modern apartments (cf. *Interiors*, vol. 115, 7 February 1956).

1908   Construction work begun for crypt at Santa Coloma; Gaudí finally retired from project in 1914.

1908–09   Project for hotel in New York (the authenticity of this project is still in doubt).

1909   Sagrada Familia schools on site of the Gloria façade.

1910   Monument to Dr. Robert erected Plaza de la Universidad, Barcelona; Gaudí's collaboration still open to question (cf. Martinell, 1975, illus. 360); 1940: dismantled and kept in storage; sculpture by Llimona; one room devoted to Gaudí's work in the exhibition of the Société Nationale des Beaux-Arts, Paris.

1911   Suffered Maltese fever; recuperation in the Pyrenees.

1911–17   Work on project for Portal of the Passion of Sagrada Familia.

1915   Crypt at Santa Coloma inaugurated.

1916   Project for Gloria façade, Sagrada Familia.

1918   Death of Eusebio Güell.

1926   June 7: Gaudí run over by a trolley bus; June 10: Gaudí died in hospital of Santa Cruz; June 12: funeral; Gaudí buried in crypt of the Sagrada Familia.

1850s	Beginnings of Renaixensa, Romantic renaissance of Catalan language and literature.
1852	First Exhibition of Industrial Products, organized by Board of Trade, Barcelona.
1859	New building in Romanesque style for Barcelona University by Elias Rogent.
1859–60	Spanish expedition in Morocco.
1860	Art and Industry Exhibition, Barcelona.
1865	Restoration of monastery at Ripoll.
1866	Birth of Francesc Berenguer.
1867	Birth of Puig i Cadafalch and of Jeroni F. Granell.
1868	Queen Isabella II of Spain deposed; Fanelli, the disciple of Bakunin, arrived in Spain.
1869	La Jove Catalunya, first Catalan society formed; Escuela Superior de Arquitectura established in Barcelona; special building erected to contain Exhibition of Industral Arts, Barcelona.
1870	Spanish Alliance of Social Democracy founded; meeting in Barcelona.
1871	The critic Sanpere y Miguel sent to study relation of art and industry in England, France and Germany; birth of Juan Rubió; plan to develop the old Barcelona Citadel into a public park.
1872	Conservatory in brick, wood and iron by Fontseré, Citadel Park.
1873	A Spanish republic declared; Doménech i Montaner qualified as architect.
1875	The Spanish monarchy restored; accession of Alfonso XII; construction of Lady Chapel at Monastery of Montserrat begun by Francisco de Paula del Villar.
1876	Publication of Verdaguer's epic Catalan poem L'Atlántida; end of second Carlist War; Catalan nationalism becomes serious; founding of Association for Catalan Scientific Excursions, ultimately (1890) The Centre for Catalan Excursions.
1877	Doménech i Montaner published article 'In Search of a National Architecture'.
1879	Birth of José Jujol; first Catalan newspaper founded, the Diari Catala, director: Almirall; foundation of Institute for the Promotion of National Work, a protectivist association of Catalan industrialists.
1880	First Conference of Catalan Nationalists; Catalan publishing house, L'Avenç, formed; appearance of Catalan newspapers, La Renaixensa and La Vanguardia.
1881	Art and Industry Exhibition (repeated 1882, 1884), Barcelona; birth of Picasso, Malaga; Doménech i Montaner elected President of Jocs Florals.
1882	Centre Catala founded; Wagner's Lohengrin presented in Barcelona; competition for façade of Barcelona's Gothic cathedral.
1883	Second Conference of Catalan Nationalism.
c. 1883	Beginnings of cultural movement in Catalonia; Modernismo: Renaixensa plus European influences.
1885	Verdaguer published Canigó, national spirited epic poem; Spanish commercial treaty with England.
1886	Almirall published outline of national ideals in Lo Catalanisme.
1887	Lliga de Catalunya founded, favouring protectionist policy.
1888	International Exhibition in Barcelona, including Doménech i Montaner's café-restaurant, now zoological museum; a Studio for Craftsmen established to promote Catalan crafts; Berenguer began hunting lodge for Güell at Garraf (1888–90).
1890	Rioting in Barcelona; demand for eight-hour working day.
1891	La Veu de Catalunya newspaper begun; anarchist bomb-thowing began in Barcelona, continuing throughout 1890s; Orfeó Catala founded, a choral group conducted by Lluís Millet.
1892	Catalonia demanded Home Rule; appearance of the political manifesto Bases de Manresa, drawn up by the newly created Unio Catalanista; Wagner's Tannhäuser produced at Liceo Theatre, Barcelona; first 'Fiesta Modernista' at Sitges (repeated 1893, 1894, 1897); Exhibition of Industrial Arts at the Bellas Artes, Barcelona; Doménech i Montaner appointed President of Unio Catalanista.
1893	Catalan Concert Society founded; Artistic Circle of St. Luke formed around Llimona; birth of Miró, Barcelona; Nietzsche's Also Sprach Zarathustra translated into Catalan.
1894	Ibsen's Enemy of the People produced in Barcelona.

1895	Maragall, Catalan poet, published *Poesies*; anarchist magazine, *Social Science*, begun; Picasso family moved to Barcelona; Doménech i Montaner's second term as President of Jocs Florals.
1896	Puig i Cadafalch built Casa Marti, Barcelona, where the café-cabaret 'Els Quatre Gats' began.
1897	Death of Elias Rogent and of Josep Fontseré.
1898	Exhibition of Applied and Fine Arts, Barcelona; first lift installed in Barcelona by Felix Cardellach; Burne-Jones and Puvis de Chavannes honoured in memorial session by Circle of St. Luke.
1899	Wagner's *Tristan und Isolde* performed in Barcelona.
1900	Lliga Regionalista formed, its mouthpiece: *La Veu de Catalunya*; its first president: Dr. Robert; a right wing party in opposition to republican 'radicals' led by Lerroux; performance of Ibsen's *Hedda Gabler*, Barcelona; Puig i Cadafalch's Casa Amatller on Paseo de Gracia, Barcelona; the magazine *Joventut* published an article on Aubrey Beardsley; Bishop of Barcelona recommended the use of Catalan in teaching the Catechism; Doménech i Montaner appointed Director of School of Architecture.
1901	Eusebio Güell established a Portland cement company; Wagner Association formed in Barcelona; Doménech i Montaner elected deputy to the Barcelona Parliament.
1902	Death of Verdaguer; general strike in Barcelona; beginnings of Syndicalist activity; Alfonso XIII succeeded to Spanish throne; Doménech i Montaner began the Hospital of St. Paul (1902–1912).
1904	Salvador Dali born at Figueras; new outbreak of bomb throwing.

1905	Last number of *La Renaixensa*.
1906	First International Congress on the Catalan Language (repeated 1913); Eugenio d'Ors founded Noucentisme movement, a return to Mediterranean classical traditions in opposition to Modernismo.
1907	Solidaridad Catalana formed mainly from the Lliga plus some republican elements to resist central government repression; Institute of Catalan Studies established; Exhibition of Fine and Applied Arts, Barcelona.
1908	Doménech i Montaner completed Palau de la Musica, Barcelona.
1909	'Tragic Sunday', fifteen days of mob rule: 'The Young Barbarians', followers of Lerroux, rebel against central government and attack the Church; 22 churches and 34 convents burnt.
1911	C.N.T. (Confederación Nacional del Trabajo) formed; organized growth of trade unionism; civil unrest.
1912	Neo-Gothic façade for Barcelona Cathedral completed.
1914	Berenguer died.
1916	Festival of United Catalonia.
1917	General strike, Barcelona.
1918	National Anarchist Conference held in Barcelona; death of Eusebio Güell.
1919	General strike, Barcelona; C.N.T. declared illegal.
1921	Strike in metallurgical industry.
1923	Primo de Rivera proclaimed himself dictator of Spain; Jujol completed church at 'Vistabella' near Tarragona; Union Socialista de Cataluña founded.

Europe

1851–53	Ruskin, *Stones of Venice*.
1852	Lewis Cubitt, King's Cross Station, London.
1853	Bogardus's passenger elevator at New York World Fair; Titus Salt's 'Saltaire', model town.

1854–68	Viollet-le-Duc, *Dictionnaire raisonné de l'architecture française*.
1855	Coignet patented reinforced concrete floor.
1856	Birth of Louis Sullivan, Boston.

1856–68 Labrouste, Bibliothèque Nationale, Paris.

1857 Safety lift by Otis installed in New York department store; birth of Charles Voysey.

1859 Butterfield completed All Saints Margaret Street Church, London; Webb, The Red House, Bexley Heath, for William Morris.

1861 William Morris-Marshall and Faulkner Company established; birth of Horta (Belgium).

1863 Birth of van de Velde (Belgium); W. H. Barlow, St. Pancras Station, London; Viollet-le-Duc, *Entretiens sur l'architecture* (1st series).

1865 Gilbert Scott, St. Pancras Station and Hotel, London; death of Joseph Paxton.

1867 Birth of Guimard (France).

1868 Birth of Mackintosh (Scotland).

1869 Birth of Frank Lloyd Wright (America).

1870 Brooklyn Bridge, New York; Krupps's work people's colonies, Essen.

1871–72 Saulnier, Menier Chocolate Factory, Noisiel-sur-Marne.

1871–73 Butterfield, Keble College, Oxford.

1872 Viollet-le-Duc, *Entretiens sur l'architecture* (2nd series).

1875 Completion of Garnier's Opéra, Paris.

1876 Eiffel and Boileau, Bon-Marché Store, Paris.

1877 Norman Shaw appointed to develop Bedford Park Suburb, London.

1878 Jenney, first Leiter Building, Chicago.

1879 Death of Viollet-le-Duc.

1880 Peabody Trust Housing, London.

1881 Sedille, Le Printemps Department Store, Paris (completed 1889).

1881–82 Forth Bridge, cantilevered steel.

1882 Mackmurdo founded Century Guild (England).

1883 Mackmurdo, title page to book, *Wren's City Churches*; birth of Gropius (Germany).

1883–85 Jenney, Home Insurance Building, Chicago.

1886 Birth of Mies van der Rohe (Germany).

1887 Birth of Le Corbusier (Switzerland) and of Mendelsohn (Germany).

1887–90 Adler and Sullivan, Auditorium Building, Chicago.

1888 Birth of Rietveld (Holland).

1889 Camillo Sitte's book on urban planning, *Der Städtebau*; Dutert and Contamin, Hall of Machines, Paris World Fair; Eiffel Tower; Jenney, second Leiter Building, Chicago.

1890 Sullivan, Wainwright Building, St. Louis; London County Council established to provide working class housing.

1891 Aston Webb's Victoria and Albert Museum completed; Burnham and Root, Monadnock Building, Chicago.

1892 Sullivan, *Ornament in Architecture*; Hennebique reinforced concrete system used in house at Bourg-la-Reine.

1893 Victor Horta, Tassel House, Brussels; Voysey, 'Perrycroft', Cornwall; *Studio* magazine begun, London.

1894 Baudot, Saint Jean de Montmartre, Paris; Otto Wagner, lectures on *Moderne Architectur* at Vienna Academy.

1894–95 Sullivan, Guarantee Building, Buffalo.

1894–98 Guimard, Castle Beranger, Paris.

1895 Bentley, Westminster Cathedral, London; Horta, Hôtel Solvay, Brussels; Guimard quoted Viollet's oblique metal columns in Ecole du Sacre Coeur, Paris; development of Bournville Garden City, near Birmingham; Burnham, Reliance Building, Chicago; Townsend, Whitechapel Art Gallery, London.

1896 Van de Velde, house at Uccle, Belgium; Messel, Wertheim Store, Berlin; Bing opened Art Nouveau Shop, Paris; death of William Morris.

1897 Founding of Vienna Secession; Hankar, 48 Rue Defacqz, Brussels; Horta, Maison du Peuple, Brussels; Endell, Studio Elvira, Munich.

1897–99 Mackintosh, Glasgow Art School.

1898 Ebenezer Howard, *A Peaceful Path to Real Reform*; Hankar, Kleyer House, Brussels; Olbrich, Secession Gallery, Vienna; Mackintosh, Cranston Street Tea Rooms, Glasgow; Hoffmann, sketch for entrance (project).

1898–1903 Berlage, Stock Exchange, Amsterdam.

1899 Garden City Association founded, London; Voysey, 'The Orchard', Chorley Wood.

1899–1904 Sullivan, Carson, Pirie and Scott Store, Chicago.

1900 Mackintosh, room for Vienna Secession and 'Windyhill' House, Kilmacolm; Guimard, Paris Metro stations; Schöllkopf, Hôtel Guilbert, Paris; de Fleure, Art Nouveau Pavilion, Paris International Exhibition.

1900–02 Townsend, Horniman Museum, London.

1901 Tony Garnier began Cité Industrielle designs (published 1918); Olbrich, Pavilion of Plastic Arts, Darmstadt.

1902	Raimondo D'Aronco, rotunda at Turin Exhibition; Perret, flats in Rue Franklin, Paris; Guimard, Hôtel de Nozal, Paris.
1903	Wiener Werkstatte formed; Unwin and Parker developed Letchworth Garden City, England; Mackintosh, Hill House, Helensburgh.
1904	Frank Lloyd Wright, Larkin Building, Buffalo.
1905	Hoffmann, Palais Stoclet, Brussels; Mackintosh, Willow Tea Rooms, Glasgow; Perret, Ponthieu Garage, Paris; Wagner, Post Office, Vienna.
1906	Frank Lloyd Wright, Unity Church, Oak Park.
1907	Mackintosh, library for Glasgow School of Art; Lutyens and Baillie Scott, Hampstead Garden Suburb, London; Deutscher Werkbund formed, Munich; Loos, Kärntner Bar, Vienna.
1908	Olbrich, Hochzeitsturm, Darmstadt; Poelzig, water mill, Breslau; Maillart developed mushroom slab construction; Behrens, A.E.G. Turbine Factory, Berlin; Loos, *Ornament and Crime*.
1908–09	Frank Lloyd Wright, Robie House and Roberts House, River Forest.
1909	First German garden city, Hellerau.
1910	Poelzig, water tower, Posen; Loos, Steiner House, Vienna; Bruno Paul developed 'Typenmöbl', mass produced furniture.
1911	Gropius and Meyer, Fagus Factory, Alfeld; Muthesius lectures, delivered at Deutsche Werkbund, on standardization.
1912	Van der Meij, Scheepvaarthuis, Amsterdam.
1912–13	Max Berg, Centenary Hall, Breslau.
1913	Rudolph Steiner, *Goetheanum* (1), Dornach, Switzerland; de Klerk, Eigenhaard Housing Estate, Amsterdam.
1914	Deutsche Werkbund Exhibition, Cologne, including Bruno Taut's glass pavilion and Gropius and Mayer's model factory; Scheerbart, *Glasarchitectur;* exhibition of Futurist architecture at Milan: Saint' Elia and Chiatone; D.I.N. Format (Deutsche Industrie Normen) established; Frank Lloyd Wright, Midway Gardens, Chicago; Le Corbusier, 'domino' housing scheme.
1914–15	Mendelsohn, architectural sketches.
1915	Garnier, Stadium, Lyons; Design and Industries Association established, London.
1916	Freyssinet, parabolic aircraft hangar, Orly; Le Corbusier, house at Chaux-des-Fonds; Van T'Hoff, Huis ter Heide, Utrecht.
1916–17	Mackintosh, Derngate, Northampton.
1917	Oud, housing project, Scheveningen, Holland; formation of De Stijl group, Holland; de Klerk, Zaanstraat Housing Estate, Amsterdam; Poelzig, House of Friendship project, Istanbul.
1917–22	Frank Lloyd Wright, Imperial Hotel, Tokyo.
1919	Bauhaus School established, Weimar; Oud, Purmerand factory project; Taut, *Alpine Architecture*; Mies van der Rohe, glass skyscraper project; Poelzig, Grosses Schauspielhaus, Berlin.
1919–21	Mendelsohn, Einstein Tower, Berlin; Le Corbusier, 'Citrohan' houses.
1920	Tatlin, Monument to the third International.
1920–25	*L'Esprit Nouveau* magazine expounding 'purist' ideas of Corbusier and Ozenfant.
1922	Gropius and Meyer, Chicago Tribune Tower project; manifesto of the Constructivist International; Mies van der Rohe, design for brick built country house; van Doesburg and Eesteren, project for 'Neo-Plastic' house.
1922–23	Perret, Notre-Dame du Raincy.
1923	Le Corbusier, *Vers une architecture*; Bauhaus exhibition: 'Art and Technics—A New Unity'.
1924	Rietveld, Schroeder House, Utrecht; death of Sullivan; Mendelsohn, hat factory at Luckenwalde.
1925	Le Corbusier, Pavilion of L'Esprit Nouveau, Exhibition of Decorative Arts, Paris; Gropius, new Bauhaus Building, Dessau.
1925–28	Steiner, *Goetheanum* (2), Dornach.
1926	Mendelsohn, Universum Cinema, Berlin; Loos, Tristan Tzara House, Paris; Le Corbusier, house at Garches.
1927	Weissenhof Exhibition, Stuttgart.

Bibliography

This is a highly selective bibliography, limiting itself mainly to works in English. Publications in foreign languages are included when they are referred to in the text or considered too important to omit. For more detailed bibliographical information consult Papers X: *Antonio Gaudí and the Catalan Movement (1870–1930)*, published by the American Association of Architectural Bibliographers (1973), compiled by George R. Collins and Maurice E. Farinas and edited by William B. O'Neal. This will remain definitive for some time.

Gaudí and his Work

R. Banham, 'The Return Curve': (Gaudí and Corbusier), *Motif*, no. 6 (1961).

J. Bassegoda and J. M. Garrut Roma, *Guia de Gaudí*. Barcelona, 1970. A very practical, tri-lingual guide book, includes chronology and description of items in the Gaudí Museum.

J. M. Bergós, *Antoni Gaudí: l'home i l'obra*. Barcelona, 1954 (revised edition, 1974).

E. Burckhardt, 'The Unfinished Cathedral and Antonio Gaudí', *Art News*, vol. 59 (January 1958).

E. Casanelles, *Antonio Gaudí: A Reappraisal*. London, 1967.

J. E. Cirlot, *The Genesis of Gaudian Architecture*. New York, 1967. Useful mainly for illustrations.

G. R. Collins, *Antonio Gaudí*. London, 1960. A most useful short introduction.

G. R. Collins, 'Gaudí, Structure and Form', *Perspecta*, no. 8 (1963), pp. 63–90.

G. R. Collins, 'The Transfer of Thin Masonry Vaulting from Spain to America', *Journal of the Society of Architectural Historians*, vol. 28 (October 1968).

Le Corbusier, *Gaudí*. Barcelona, 1967.

S. Dali, 'De la beauté terrifiante et comestible de l'architecture modern style', *Minotaure*, no. 3-4 (1933).

R. Descharnes, 'Gaudí, le héros espagnol de l'architecture 1900 a aussi fait des meubles', *Connaissance des Arts*, no. 228 (February 1971).

R. Descharnes and C. Prevost, *Gaudí the Visionary*. Lausanne, 1971. An over-elaborate publication, translated from the French, but useful for including a recent article by Dali and a discussion of Gaudí's sculptural methods.

J. M. Garrut Roma, 'Gaudí en la caricatura', *San Jorge Barcelona*, no. 37 (January 1960).

C. Giedion Welcker, *Park Güell*. Barcelona, 1966.

H. R. Hitchcock, *Gaudí*. New York, 1957–58. Catalogue of exhibition at the Museum of Modern Art, New York.

H. R. Hitchcock, 'The Work of Antoni Gaudí i Cornet', *Architectural Association Journal*, no. 74 (1958).

Illustrated London News: 17 December 1927, 10 March 1928, 23 February 1929.

J. Jürgen, 'Antonio Gaudí', *Architecture d'Aujourd'hui*, vol. 33 (June/July 1962).

A. Kerrigan, 'Gaudianism in Catalonia', *Arts*, vol. 32 (December 1957).

M. Leblond, 'Gaudí et l'architecture méditerranéenne', *L'Art et les Artistes*, vol. 11 (1910).

F. Loyer, 'La Chapelle Güell', *L'OEil* (June 1971).

E. Marquina, 'La Sagrada Familia', *L'Art et les Artistes* (1908) pp. 516–22.

C. Martinell, *Gaudí*, ed. G. Collins. Cambridge, Massachusetts, 1975. Judith Rohrer's English translation of the most thorough study (Barcelona, 1967) yet produced.

J. Perucho, *Gaudí, una arquitectura de anticipación*. Barcelona, 1967. A tri-lingual study, mainly useful for illustrations.

N. Pevsner, 'The Strange Architecture of Gaudí', *The Listener* (7 August 1952).

C. Prevost, 'Comment travaillait Gaudí', *L'OEil* (June/July 1969).

J. F. Rafols, *Gaudí*. The first monograph written on Gaudí, it is the work of an assistant who had access to Gaudí's papers before the 1936 destruction and is, therefore, of fundamental importance. The first edition was published in Catalan in 1928, the second in Spanish in 1929 and the third in 1952.

J. L. Sert, *Cripta de la Colonia Güell*. Barcelona, 1969.

J. L. Sert, 'Gaudí, visionnaire et précurseur', *L'OEil* (February 1955).

P. M. Stratton, 'The Sagrada Familia', *The Builder,* vol. 133 (August 1927).

J. J. Sweeney and J. L. Sert, *Antoni Gaudí*. London, 1960.

M. Tapié, *La Pedrera*. Barcelona, 1971.

S. Tarrago, *Gaudí*. Barcelona, 1974. Excellent corpus of colour illustrations.

E. Waugh, 'Gaudí', *Architectural Review,* vol. 67 (June 1930).

Gaudí's only extensive personal writings, the diary he kept during student days and the study entitled 'Ornamentation' (1878), a confused collection of jottings and student notes, are printed in full in the Spanish version of Martinell's *Gaudí*. The English edition has selections from these manuscripts, and a shorter selection is to be found in Casanelles's *Antonio Gaudí*. Gaudí was suspicious of eloquence and disliked visitors taking notes when they went to see him. There are, however, two useful texts of such conversations: C. Martinell, *Conversaciónes con Gaudí* (Barcelona, 1969) and J. M. Bergós, 'Las conversaciónes de Gaudí', *Hogar y Arquitectura,* no. 112 (1974). A. Alvarez, 'Gaudí Speaks', *Jubilee,* vol. 9 (1962) is a short selection of Gaudí's aphorisms without references.

Gaudí in Context

Political and social context:

G. Brenan, *Spanish Labyrinth*. Cambridge, 1960.

Background of Catalan Gothic architecture:

A. Cirici and O. Maspons, *Architectura Gotica Catalana*. Barcelona, 1968.

Architecture in Barcelona:

J. E. H. Cros, G. Mora and X. Pouplana, *Architectura de Barcelona*. Barcelona, n.d.

Spanish vernacular architecture:

L. Feduchi, *Itinerarios de architectura popular española,* three volumes. Barcelona, 1974 (English translation 1975–76). The third volume deals with Catalonia.

C. Flores, *Architectura popular española*. Barcelona, 1973.

Gaudí's architectural contemporaries:

O. Bohigas, *Arquitectura modernista*. Barcelona, 1968. Excellent photographic survey with interesting essays.

O. Bohigas, 'Doménech i Montaner', *Architectural Review,* vol. 142 (December 1967). Reprinted in N. Pevsner and J. M. Richards (eds.), *The Anti-Rationalists*. London, 1973.

O. Bohigas, *Reseña y catalogo de la arquitectura modernista*. Barcelona, 1973.

M. L. Borras, *Doménech i Montaner*. Barcelona, 1971. A multi-lingual study.

E. Jardi, *Puig i Cadafalch*. Barcelona, 1975.

J. M. Jujol, *La arquitectura de J. Ma. Jujol*. Barcelona, 1974.

D. Mackay, 'Berenguer', *Architectural Review,* vol. 136 (December 1964). Reprinted in N. Pevsner and J. M. Richards (eds.), *The Anti-Rationalists*. London, 1973.

C. Pellicer, *1900 a Barcelona*. Barcelona, 1967.

I. S. M. Rubio, *Joan Rubio i Bellver y la fortuna del Gaudinismo*. Barcelona, 1975.